Spanish Pronunciation in the Americas

Spanish Pronunciation in the Americas

D. Lincoln Canfield

The University of Chicago Press

Chicago and London

The University of Chicago Press, Chicago 60637
The University of Chicago Press, Ltd., London

Library of Congress Cataloging in Publication Data

Canfield, Delos Lincoln, 1903–
    Spanish pronunciation in the Americas.

    Includes bibliographies and index.
    1.   Spanish language–Dialects–America.
    2.   Spanish language–Pronunciation.   I.   Title.
PC4821.C33   467'.973   80–23664
ISBN 0-226-09262-3
ISBN 0-226-09263-1 (pbk.)

D. LINCOLN CANFIELD is professor emeritus of
Spanish at Southern Illinois University. He is the
author of *La pronunciación del español en América;
East Meets West, South of the Border;* and *El español
a través de sus escritores* and is the editor of the
third edition of *The University of Chicago Spanish
Dictionary,* published by the University of Chicago
Press.

Contents

Preface

In the belief that there are always diachronic elements in synchronic dialectology, this study will examine the pronunciation of the Spanish of America as a manifestation of the Castilian continuum—which is in turn a direct descendant of the spoken Latin of the north-central part of the Iberian Peninsula. As in all language, the Spanish norm at any given moment is determined by what has been, and the Spanish-speaking individual is virtually forced to conform to the speech tradition of his community.

As the centuries pass, however, the accessibility of units of population in America to the original source—in this case Castilian through the ports of southern Spain—becomes an important factor in the evolution of the language (polymorphous and ever changing) in outlying places. Thus geographical differences of today have two principal parameters: accessibility and chronology. The territories that were more accessible during the colonial period have in general received later stages of an evolving phonology, while the inaccessible regions (the mountains and landlocked areas) tend to be more conservative in terms of the history of the language.

Beyond this there are also societal constraints that through social coercion have brought about "social" dialects within the geographically designated speech pattern. Age, sex, class, occupation, the urban-rural dichotomy, and other factors appear to carry associated attitudes that in turn may be represented in speech "styles." Thus I will refer to such variations within the area pattern as "attitudinal." Although much remains to be done in the examination of "attitudinal" differences, some very interesting studies have been made within the past fifteen years.

The "styles" of Mexico City Spanish based on speed of speech and the consequent degree of care in articulation have been examined by Harris (1969), and several articles on speech attitudes based on sex, age, and education have been written by the Argentine linguists Donni de Mirande (1967, 1974) and Fontanella de Weinberg (1967, 1974*a*, 1974*b*). Panamanian attitudes associated with the urban-rural dichotomy are related to habits of pronunciation by Alvarado de Ricord (1971), and in Mexico Lope Blanch (1966, 1974) and Alvar (1966–67) have studied social differences within given areas, as Zapata Arellano (1975) has done for Chile. Terrell (1977) writes of Caribbean constraints, some of which may be social.

Dialect identification becomes even more complicated when one notes that an attitudinal feature in one place may be a general feature in another. Male speakers in the Caribbean, for instance, often remind us that the careful articulation of syllable final /s/ is considered effeminate or at least affected, whereas in highland Spanish America this is the usual thing.

Moreover, one discovers that certain group differences are stages in the chronological phonology of Castilian. The woman's sibilant articulation in Buenos Aires, for instance, may be more conservative than the man's in terms of the history of Spanish, and the case will thus correspond to differences between highlands and coast in Venezuela, where accessibility during the colonial period is apparently the dialect parameter.

In conversation with a radio announcer from Valparaíso, Chile, I noted that he consciously pronounced /č/ as [š]. When questioned, he stated that he considered it "más suave." What he thought of as meticulous articulation actually involved the elimination of an occlusive element, a change that occurred in French during the thirteenth century and that is now taking place in cities of northern Chile, in Panama, in Cuba, and elsewhere.

In this study I propose first to trace briefly, with references to more extensive treatments, the development of certain phonological phenomena that seem to have created what we now call dialects of Spanish, through factors of conquest and settlement and, importantly, through the factor of accessibility during the entire colonial period of some three hundred years.

Second, the Spanish of each American region, including several regions within the United States, will be described in articulatory terms, country by country, with maps that show significant dialectal traits by region as well as can be indicated with the information available and that note any "attitudinal" differences that may have been observed. I make no claim to supply anything approaching a linguistic atlas. The only area that has been thoroughly studied is Colombia, and it will be some time before publication of the *ALEC* (*Atlas lingüístico etnográfico de Colombia*) by the Instituto Caro y Cuervo, Bogotá.

But fairly well defined regional differences are indicated in a general way by hatched maps.

Special bibliographies for each area will list important sources of data and will refer to the main Bibliography, which includes some three hundred pertinent books and articles.

The approach of the book is historical-descriptive, and the principal sources of information are historical treatises on the development of Spanish phonemes and their variants, contemporary accounts of dialectal phenomena, and my own observations, based on more than sixty years of residence, travel, research, and teaching among Spanish-speaking people representing most sections of the Hispanic world.

Since the publication of Tomás Navarro Tomás's *Cuestionario lingüístico hispanoamericano* (Buenos Aires, 1943, 1945), interest in the dialectal manifestations of American Spanish has grown apace, and many researchers have become concerned with the description of the phonology, the syntax, or the vocabulary of the varieties of Spanish spoken in the republics of Latin America and in the Spanish-speaking areas of the United States. One appreciates the scope of these investigations by consulting the *Bibliografía de la lingüística española* of Homero Serís (1964) and previous and subsequent bibliographies by Nichols, Woodbridge, Davis, Teschner, Beardsley, Canfield, Resnick, Huberman, Solé, and others, as well as the language section of the humanities volumes of the *Handbook of Latin American Studies*.

The phonological development of Spanish is well documented since 1492, and such works as the *Biblioteca histórica de la filología castellana* (Madrid, 1893), by the Conde de la Viñaza, the same writer's *Bibliografía española de lenguas indígenas de América* (Madrid, 1892), and the many books on Indian languages that emanated from the presses of Mexico and Peru during the colonial period reveal to some extent the philological interests of Spaniards over the years.

We now have special studies of most of the republics of Spanish America, or at least of parts of their territories, as well as of the four main Spanish-speaking sections of the United States (the Mexican border, northern New Mexico/southern Colorado, Florida, and New York City and other urban centers of the Northeast). For Argentina, Colombia, and Mexico, where centers of linguistic investigations are situated, books and articles have been written describing aspects of the Spanish of each, and much of the recent research has been rather carefully and objectively done.

My own experience includes living and playing with Mexicans of the Arizona/Sonora border while I was between the ages of twelve and sixteen, twenty summers of tour-conducting to Mexico and Guatemala, a consultantship at the Universidad Nacional Autónoma de México, a visiting professorship at the Universidad de San Carlos in Guatemala, a Fulbright senior lectureship in Hispanic linguistics at the Instituto Caro y Cuervo, Bogotá, Colombia, a research grant in linguistics at the Universidad de San Salvador, and five NDEA summer teaching assignments in Mexico and one in Guatemala. I have made on-the-spot recordings in Mexico, Guatemala, El Salvador, Honduras, Colombia (including recordings of *quiteños* studying in Bogotá), Peru, Chile, Argentina (only in Buenos Aires), Venezuela, and Puerto Rico, and I have also made recordings in the United States of visiting Bolivians, Panamanians, Cubans, Costa Ricans, and residents of other areas where I have not yet gone.

Origins of American Spanish

In number of speakers, Spanish is the largest manifestation of spoken Latin. Those who now think and express themselves in Castilian, or Spanish, number more than 200,000,000 and live in some twenty countries. Moreover, one section of this language community, Latin America, has one of the fastest-growing populations of the world. It is estimated that by A.D. 2000 Spanish will be the language of some 400,000,000 persons and may very well be spoken by more people than any other language except Mandarin Chinese.

Castilian Latin, now referred to as Spanish in most parts of the world, but known as *castellano* in several of the Spanish-speaking regions, became prominent because of the hegemony of north-central Spain in the reconquest of the Iberian Peninsula from the Moors. It grew and took form as Castilian under conditions of coexistence with Semitic peoples, and its predominance among other forms of spoken Latin is due not to intrinsic value, but rather to extralinguistic factors: political and military power and organization, church-state relations, literary ascendancy, and a very successful acculturation of other peoples, principally through intermarriage.

The conquest and colonization of America by the Spaniards developed with vertiginous rapidity for that period, in a climate of religiosity and nationalism. Many of the Spanish explorers showed up in several parts of the vast territory of America during their adventurous lives. Lines of communication were tenuous, so that in contrast to the United States, where frontiers moved forward slowly but solidly, Spanish settlements generally were widely scattered.

Points in America that were thousands of miles apart were settled at the same time and were endowed with the same stage of Hispanic culture and language through the same ports of southern Spain. For this reason we do not have neat isoglosses of structural features on the total American scene, and an attempt to depict linguistic zones in America would produce a leopardlike picture. For example, at least

1

two dialectal features of Costa Rica are also to be found in western Argentina, and things thought of as Mexican are also heard in Bolivia. Vladimir Honsa (1975) has shown how complicated the zoning attempt becomes. On the other hand, lines and zones can be indicated within today's national boundaries.

With all this in mind, it becomes apparent that the chief factor in the development of dialectal differences has been accessibility during the period 1500–1800—accessibility to changes that were taking place in the Spanish of southern Spain. The phonology of highland Bolivia is much more conservative than that of Cuba or even the llanos of Bolivia.

Swayed by a crusading spirit brought about by hundreds of years of struggle with the Mohammedans, the church took a leading part in the acculturation of the American Indian. In an atmosphere of religious fanaticism, Cortés and other captains of conquest became agents of the faith, while the clergy became instruments of the state, both insisting on the conversion as well as the submission of the natives. The Spanish of America still bears the seal of strong church influence, especially in its lexicon and idiom.

The fundamental traits of American Spanish, as I have indicated, are to be found in Castilla—the language is Castilian. But, as Castilian was taken to southern Spain with the Reconquest, certain changes began to evolve in its structure that ultimately created what has been referred to as the Andalusian dialect of Castilian, with its focal point in Seville but with extensive settlements from there in Extremadura and in Granada (Navarro 1933).

Records reveal that nearly all early expeditions sailed from southern ports: Seville, Huelva, Palos, Málaga, and Cádiz. And with the publication of Peter Boyd-Bowman's *Indice geobiográfico de 40,000 pobladores españoles de América en el siglo XVI, 1493–1519* (vol. 1, 1964; vol. 2, 1968) we have for the first time a rather detailed analysis of the peninsular origins of the Spanish settlers of America, although the author had given a preview in *PMLA* (1956). Boyd-Bowman used data from many sources, including much information from the Archivo de Indias of Seville: extensive passenger lists and *papeletas* that show not only where the settler was from, but where he went in America, what his trade or profession was, and who went with him. These findings reveal the strong Andalusian influence during the first century and a half of colonization.

The features and the tendencies of selection of the Andalusian dialect seem to have become established in America beginning about 1500, but the process was very slow. The transcriptions of several distinct Indian languages during the first half of the sixteenth century, mostly by Spaniards who were born in the late fifteenth century, reveal a phonology like that of Antonio de Nebrija and not different from that of Toledo (Canfield 1934, 1952). As time passed, the areas of America that were accessible to traffic and intercourse with the ports of southern Spain, and with points farther north through these ports, seem to have been affected most by selections that were being made in an evolving pattern of polymorphous phonemes—the Andalusian dialect. Fewer of the changes that were to occur during the next two hundred years reached the inaccessible regions of America.

In the meantime, the Castilian of northern and central Spain, while retaining most of the traits of the pre-Columbian period, underwent changes and levelings, some of which were shared by the South and hence by America. But one, the development of [θ] for a former [s] (orthographic *ç, z, c* before *e, i*) never became an American style, and in southern Spain it exists in a weakened form as part of a polymorphous sibilant situation. Spaulding and Patt (1949) believe that the interdental articulation was the usual one by 1700.

Before the northern/southern dichotomy of about 1500, selections were made in the phonological pattern of Castilian, mostly in the form of leveling of a pair of phonemes to one: the unvoicing of the voiced intervocalic sibilants, which made them coincide with the voiceless ones that already existed. *Oso* [ożo] and *osso* [oṡo] were leveled to [oṡo]; *hazes* [házeṡ] and *haces* [háseṡ] became phonetically [háseṡ], later [áseṡ]; *xira* [šíra] *(banquete)* and *gira* [ǰíra] or [žíra] leveled to [šíra]. This unvoicing apparently started early in the far North and extended finally to the South during the sixteenth century, then to America, where today there are still vestiges of the original voicing in Ecuador's highlands and in the Department of Nariño in Colombia.

Two other developments that eliminated phonemes were taking place in the North during the late Middle Ages or even earlier: *b* [b] and *v* [v] or [ƀ] were simplified to one /b/, with allophones [b] (initial in breath group or after nasal) and [ƀ] elsewhere. But in several areas of America the occlusive is heard today not only initially and after a nasal but after any consonant or semivowel. Before the loss of the phoneme /v/, *cabe* was [kábe] and *cave* was [káve] or [káƀe]. The *h* [h] from Latin F (probably pronounced bilabially in the North) gradually disappeared in the North and finally elsewhere, although today there are many vestiges of the strong aspiration in southern Spain and in Spanish America.

An interesting observation of some of these levelings is to be found in the work of Fray Juan de Córdoba, *Arte de la lengua zapoteca* (Mexico, 1578) (Canfield 1952). While discussing regional differences in Zapoteca, Córdoba writes: "Porque entre nosotros y en nuestra España es lo mesmo que los de Castilla la Vieja dizen hacer, y en Toledo hazer, y dizen xugar, y en toledo jugar, y dizen yerro y en Toledo hierro. Y dizen alagar y en Toledo halagar, y otros muchos vocablos que dexo por euitar prolixidad." Fray Juan was born about 1500, probably in Toledo. Incidentally, his transcriptions of Zapoteca, which has both voiced and voiceless sibilants, revealed, among other things, a set of four sibilants ([s, z, š, ž]) in his own Spanish beyond /ś/ and /ż/, which he did not find in Zapoteca.

These pre-Columbian changes ultimately reached southern Spain and, through the southern ports, America, and there was yet another that apparently reached maturity about 1650: the [š], which had traditionally been represented orthographically by *x*, and the [ž] which had been written *j* and *g* (*e, i*) coalesced to [š], first in the North, as Juan de Córdoba has indicated, then in Toledo, the South, and America. By a century later the palatal sibilant had become velar in most of the Spanish-speaking world, although regionally its manifestations range from uvular to laryngeal. It is very likely that the original [š] was actually retroflex, similar to that of Nahuatl or Russian, or it may have been a set of two fricatives (two sets of vibrations).

It was about 1500 that another leveling apparently started in southern Spain—one that was not shared by the North but eventually was shared by America. Testimony to this shows up in occasional spellings and in a phrase used by some of Spain's chroniclers: "Ceceaba como sevillano." Since, according to the research of Spaulding and Patt (1949), there was no interdental generally until nearly 1700, this could only mean that the "guilty" party's sibilant articulation was thought of as *ce* for both [s] and [ś]. Indications are that Spanish had an apicoalveolar /ś/ from Latin S, and a dental or dorsoalveolar /s/—written *ç, z, c* (*e, i*), the *z* being used syllable final. The *sevillano* was beginning to level them to the one involving the less physical effort, [s], and with time this tendency became the usual American one (exceptions are to be found in Antioquia, Colombia, and highland Bolivia, where the selection of the apicoalveolar as the surviving phoneme evidently took place rather early). Generally, however, the so-called *seseo* of America is actually a *ceceo* historically (Canfield 1934/1962*a*; Lapesa 1956, 1964). Cock Hincapié (1969) demonstrates that there was considerable evidence of leveling in the Nuevo Reino de Granada between 1550 and 1650. Such a work as the *Nueva crónica y buen gobierno,* of Felipe Guaman Poma de Ayala, written between 1587 and 1615 by a man who was born about 1535, shows confusion of the sibilants in Peru (edition of Luis F. Bustios Gálvez, Lima: Ministerio de Educación Pública del Perú, 1956). In Mexico the early missionaries from Spain had observed a strict distinction between [s] (*ç* or -*z*) and [ś] (*s* or *ss*) in their transcriptions and often spoke of *s* as "una letra que falta," but the *criollo* writers of the late sixteenth century use the sibilants almost indiscriminately in describing [s] of a native language and wonder why the original priests had used *c*.

Several other phonological developments of southern Spain were taken to America by successive waves of *pobladores* during some two hundred years after 1600. Although more and more Spaniards came to America from the far North of Spain during the eighteenth, nineteenth, and twentieth centuries, in a generation or two these *gallegos, asturianos,* and *vascos* evidently adapted through social coercion to the American pattern of southern Spanish origin.

An examination of the *andalucismos* of a phonological character that are now a part of American Spanish reveals that they are aspects of a general trend in articulation that one might call *lenguaplana*, a lessening of muscular tension in grooving for sibilants and in tongue-raising for alveolar and palatal articulations, all of which may correspond to an attitude of less effort.

The apicoalveolar /ś/ was lost in southern Spain and in America when there was less effort to raise the tongue to the concave position, and with time even the muscular tension involved in grooving has been lost in many areas. Finally, the /s/ syllable final becomes only an aspiration or disappears. According to Fontanella de Weinberg (1974*a*) and Terrell (1977), the -/s/ is deleted more in the speech of the lower economic groups of Argentina and the Caribbean than in the "educated" elements of society, and this has been the observation of many others.

Two American Spanish phenomena that seem to go back to the time of the early settlements are, first, the occlusive articulation of /b/, /d/, /g/ under conditions where they are fricative in "standard" Spanish and, second, the so-called *seseo*.

In the stream of speech of Colombia (except Nariño), El Salvador, Honduras, and Nicaragua, the occlusive allophone of the consonants /b/, /d/, /g/ is heard after any consonant or semivowel. In on-the-spot recordings of more than one hundred persons that I made during the summers of 1951 and 1952 (Canfield 1960*a*), the only deviation from this norm was in a person from the border of Guatemala. Recordings made in Tegucigalpa had the same pattern, but the coast of Honduras may be a different story. Lacayo (1954) noted the same consistency in Nicaragua, as I did (Canfield 1962*b*) during six months of teaching at the Instituto Caro y Cuervo, Bogotá, with trips to many parts of the country. Albor (1971), who is from Barranquilla and has studied in Bogotá and in the United States, describes the fricatives of Nariño Spanish in contrast to his own occlusives. Resnick (1976) rightly points out that nonstandard occlusive pronunciations are common in many regions other than those noted, but it has been my observation that, although recordings reveal occlusives where not expected in some speakers from Ecuador, Bolivia, Guatemala, and Costa Rica, they do not show the consistent pattern of the four countries indicated. Many nonstandard occlusives are heard in the Caribbean area, where there has been leveling of -/r/ and -/l/, and even -/s/ (*desde* [dédde]; *verdad* [beddá]). Where the occlusive is consistent after another consonant or a semivowel, the phrase *las barbas* is heard as [laz bárbas] or [laḥ bárbah], depending on the treatment of /s/ syllable final in that region. In Madrid it would be [laż ƀárƀaš] and, in Mexico City or Lima, [laz ƀárƀas].The phrase *Se ve muy verde esta tarde* is heard as [se ƀe mwi bérde ésta tárde], *Margarita ha dicho algo* is [margaríta a ɟíčo álgo], and *El buey volvió* becomes [el bwéj bolbjó].

As I have indicated, the Spanish missionaries and chroniclers who came to America immediately after the conquests—even the southerners—seem to have had three sets of sibilants: /s/, /z/; /ś/, /ż/; /š/, /ž/ (*cinco, hazer; classe, casa; dexar, viaje*), and apparently those from the North had lost the voiced/voiceless distinction, so that *osso* and *oso* were both [óśo]; but as I have noted, a further coalescence took place during the sixteenth century, beginning in Andalusia. Popular opinion would have it that the Spanish American has lost his /θ/. Actually, there was no interdental well established until long after American Spanish had an identity as such. The sibilant ancestor of the /θ/ is the [s] that is heard in nearly all of Spanish America, with various degrees of muscular tension, and the phoneme that was lost was the /ś/ [ś], so characteristic of Spanish throughout recorded history, and still one of a pair, /s/ and /θ/, in all but southern Spain. The [θ] of Spain had been [ts] in the remote Middle Ages, so the sibilant of America represents an intermediate stage in an evolution of centuries.

Yet another manifestation of the *lenguaplana* mode is the leveling of the two phonemes /ļ/ and /y/, which apparently began in the middle of the seventeenth century and for some reason was first associated with urban centers of southern Spain and Spanish America. It is now gaining ground in central Spain and sections of America (Chile, for instance). Nevertheless, in vast areas of America /ļ/ and /y/ are still distinguished: *valla* from *vaya,* and *halla* from *haya.* This is true in

Bolivia, most of Peru, Paraguay, Ecuador's highlands (in two different ways), and much of the Eastern Cordillera of Colombia, although it is weakening generationally in Bogotá, Pasto, and other cities, and in regions of northern Argentina (in two different ways).

One of the latest (in terms of the colonial period) results of the *lenguaplana* vogue is the lax articulation of the /r/ syllable final, in that the single vibration is not completed, leading to an acoustical equivalence with /l/. The phonetic outcome at times resembles [r] and at times [l], and it often is difficult to identify as either. The tendency is very apparent in Puerto Rico, the Dominican Republic, Venezuela, Panama, central Chile, coastal Colombia, and to a growing extent in Cuba. Southern Spain is apparently the source (*ALPI* 1: 39).

Although there seem to be no indications of the phenomenon in the colonial period, one of the most extended traits in American Spanish today is the velar /n/ [ŋ] as a sign of word finality. *Enamora* is [enamóra], but *en amor* is [eŋ amór] in much of southern Spain and in sections of America. English-speakers and Germans who hear this nasal for the first time think of *ng* (*sing*). Since Spanish has one word-final nasal phoneme, *swing* and *swim* may be homophonous to certain speakers of Spanish. The *velar* is common before an initial vowel in a following word or before a pause, but it often intrudes unexpectedly: *anhelo* [aŋélo]. Recent research tends to indicate that in many cases the nasal is neither velar nor alveolar but rather a nasalization of the final vowel. Terrell (1975*b*) has found this to be true in Cuba and has compared the frequency of occurrence with that in Panama and Puerto Rico. The velar /n/ word final before a following vowel or before a pause is common in southern Mexico, all of Central America, coastal Colombia, most of Venezuela, Cuba, Puerto Rico, the Dominican Republic, Peru, Ecuador, and Bolivia. In the last three countries the velar nasal may be reinforced by the velar nasal of Quechua.

Perhaps the only outstanding feature of American Spanish that is not traceable to Andalusia is the assibilation of /r̄/ ([ř]). This tendency has been called Bogotá *r*, Guatemalan *r*, Costa Rican *r*, and so forth, and has been ascribed to the influence of Indian languages. As a matter of fact, it is heard in probably half the Spanish-speaking territory of America. In some places, notably Guatemala, it is often voiceless and is confused with /s/ by outsiders: *la ropa*, as pronounced by many people in Guatemala, sounds to a Spaniard like *la sopa*, and the [ř̥] is almost identical to the apicoalveolar [ŝ] of central and northern Spain. Palatographic and spectrographic analyses show them to be very much alike, with perhaps a little more length in the Spanish [ŝ]. Final /r/ and even preconsonantal /r/ in this same pattern are often assibilated, so that *decir,* as pronounced by millions of Spanish Americans, especially women and men of *fino hablar,* has two distinct sibilants [desís]. The case that is noticed most is the combination /tr/, which, by becoming alveolar in both elements, takes on an acoustic similarity to [č], and *tronco* sounds like *chonco* to the uninitiated. I recall a resident of Guatemala City who always referred to the *parque* as [páške].

Although the assibilation is rare in Spain today (*ALPI,* vol. 1), it is very common in New Mexico, Guatemala, Costa Rica, eastern highland Colombia, highland Ecuador, Bolivia's highlands, Chile, western and northern Argentina, and Paraguay. It is also noted to a lesser extent in Mexico and Peru. Although it is not possible to produce evidence of the Andalusian origin of the phenomenon of assibilation, that it seems to be most common in the less accessible regions seems to indicate that it may have been a feature of sixteenth- or seventeenth-century Spanish.

One of the elements of confusion and limitation in the recorded history of the Spanish of America has been the practice of so many writers of describing the language of their own region without much knowledge of Spanish as spoken in other parts of Spanish America, giving the impression that the local traits are unique, whereas actually the phenomena they depict may exist in identical form two thousand miles away. *Argentinismos, mexicanismos, panameñismos* often turn out to be *americanismos,* but with scattered occurrence.

Beset by these concerns and by the tendency of some writers to try to create neat zones, Melvyn Resnick (1975) decided to cast aside taxonomic considerations and look at all the available data on phonological variants in the total area. Then, by using distinctive feature techniques of discrimination, he proceeded to break down the entire corpus into binarily specifiable units of information, which, by the presence or absence of a feature, create a dialect. Each distinction in theory automatically makes two "dialects." By a clever use of two basic tables, the author numbered more than two hundred "dialects" that are associated with countries, regions, cities, levels of society, age, or mood of expression. Although the principal thrust of his treatise is methodological, by illustration Resnick has produced an extensive document of many variations in American Spanish phonology and at the same time demonstrated that similarities do exist between widely separated places and that there are vertical as well as horizontal parameters in Hispanic dialectology.

THE SPANISH SIMPLEX

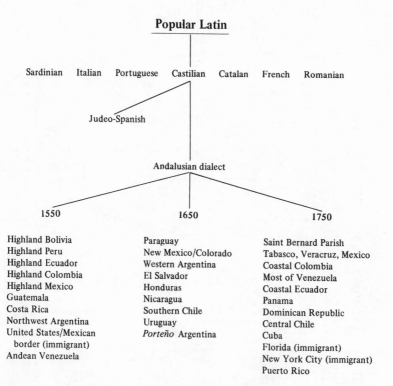

Popular Latin

Sardinian   Italian   Portuguese   Castilian   Catalan   French   Romanian

Judeo-Spanish

Andalusian dialect

1550	1650	1750
Highland Bolivia	Paraguay	Saint Bernard Parish
Highland Peru	New Mexico/Colorado	Tabasco, Veracruz, Mexico
Highland Ecuador	Western Argentina	Coastal Colombia
Highland Colombia	El Salvador	Most of Venezuela
Highland Mexico	Honduras	Coastal Ecuador
Guatemala	Nicaragua	Panama
Costa Rica	Southern Chile	Dominican Republic
Northwest Argentina	Uruguay	Central Chile
United States/Mexican	*Porteño* Argentina	Cuba
border (immigrant)		Florida (immigrant)
Andean Venezuela		New York City (immigrant)
		Puerto Rico

This chart represents in rather simplified form the Latin origin of Spanish as spoken in America, its previous peninsular development from north to south, and the American results of successive changes in its Andalusian manifestation. Shown also is the fact that Spanish, or Castilian, is a simplex in that its manifestations are mutually intelligible. The speech of Italy is a complex of Latin *languages*. As noted in the text, accessible regions tend to represent the latest developments.

9

PRINCIPAL PHONETIC MANIFESTATIONS OF THE PHONEMES OF SPANISH

	Bilabial		Labiodental		Interdental		Dental		Alveolar		Palatal		Velar		Glottal	
Voice	vs	vd	vs	vd	vs	vd	vs	vd	vs	vd	vs	vd	vs	vd	vs	vd
Occlusive	p	b					t	d					k	g	ʔ	
Slit fricative	ɸ	β	f	v	θ	đ	θ				x́	y	x	ǥ	h	ḥ
Grooved fricative							s	z	ṡ, r̝̊, r̝̊	ż, r̝, r̝	š	ž				
Lateral										l		ĺ				
Affricate									t͡s		č, t͡ĵ	ŷ, (ɟ)				
Nasal		m						n̪		n		ñ		ŋ		
Vibrant									r̥	r, r̄			R̥	R		
Semiconsonant		w										j				

Notes: 1. Owing to extensive polymorphism in American Spanish, the place of articulation may not be exact for some dialects.
2. Because of phonemic considerations, [ɹ̝] and [R] are listed as vibrants. They are usually slit fricatives, close to the [x] of Spain.
3. The [x] of Spain (except the South) is usually uvular. This is rare in America.

THE CONSONANTAL PHONEMES OF AMERICAN SPANISH
WITH SOME PHONETIC VARIANTS

/p/: [p] *papa, copa, prado.*

/b/: [b] initially in breath group and after a nasal, *bomba* [bómba]; ƀ elsewhere, *cabe* [káƀe], *cave* [káƀe], *la vaca* [la ƀáka], *la barba* [la ƀárƀa], *alba* [álƀa]. Exceptions: [b] after another consonant or after a semivowel in Colombia (except Nariño), El Salvador, Honduras, Nicaragua, and sporadically in the Andes and in the Caribbean.

/t/: [t] *todo, cometa.*

/d/: [d] initially in breath group and after /n/ and /l/ (*donde, falda*); đ elsewhere, with a strong tendency toward deletion between vowels and word final: [merkáo], [usté]. Preserved most in highland Mexico, Guatemala, Ecuador, Peru, and Bolivia, and in Nariño, Colombia. In El Salvador, Honduras, Nicaragua, Colombia (except Nariño), and in Caribbean areas where -/l/, -/r/ and even -/s/ are acoustically equivalent, [d] is usual after another consonant or semivowel: *pardo* [párdo]; *desde* [désde] or [déhde]; *rey de copas* [r̄ej de kópas].

/k/: [k] *aquí, cosa;* for /p/ in *combinaciones cultas* [sektjémbre] [konseksjón] in Colombia, Central America, Venezuela, sporadically in the Caribbean and elsewhere; *boca* is often bóʔa in sections of Colombia's north Pacific coast.

/g/: [g] initially in breath group and after a nasal [ŋ]; ǥ elsewhere, *la garra, algo, pargo.* Exceptions: in El Salvador, Honduras, Nicaragua, Colombia (not Nariño), it is [g] after any consonant or semivowel: *la guerra* [la ǥér̄a] but *hay guerra* [aj gér̄a]. Tendency toward [g] in areas where -/l/, -/r/, and even -/s/ are acoustically equivalent.

/f/: [f] in careful urban speech, but more often [ɸ] in much of America.

/s/: [s] *solo, casa, caza, ves, vez* [sólo] [kása] [kása] [bes] [bes]. Often [ṡ] in Antioquia and Caldas, Colombia, and frequent in Bolivia's altiplano. Often [θ] in El Salvador, Honduras, Nicaragua, and some coastal areas of Venezuela, Colombia, and Ecuador; *las manos, los dados, las barbas* [laz mános] | [loz đáđos] [laz ƀárƀas] ([z] before a voiced consonant or semiconsonant) but at least as often [lah mánoh] in vast coastal areas of America, in most of Venezuela, the llanos of Bolivia, in Paraguay, much

11

of the interior of Argentina, and in the northern New Mexico/ southern Colorado dialect region.

/y/: [ŷ] initially or after /n/ and /l/ and after /s/ in some regions where -/s/ is aspirated; [y] intervocalically, but [ž] in Buenos Aires and southeast Argentina and Uruguay; [ŷ] generally in Paraguay and in Antioquia, Colombia; [i̯] generally in Mexican border Spanish (including Monterrey, N.L., Mexico) as well as all of Central America and coastal areas of Venezuela, Colombia, and Ecuador. Orthographic *ll* represents the same phoneme, except in Paraguay, highland Peru, all of Bolivia, highland Ecuador, and the Eastern Cordillera of Colombia, where the traditional phonemic distinction between /l̮/ and /y/ still exists, either as [bál̮a-báya] or as [báža-báya].

/x/: [x] in most of Mexico; in Chile and the River Platte region; in the Andes, most of the area except Bolivia. In the Caribbean, in most of Central America, Panama, Colombia, and Venezuela, it is [h]. In no region of America is it uvular as in central and northern Spain. Chile's *gente* is [çénte].

/č/: [č] *chato, mucho* [čáto] [múčo], but in the younger generation of Panama's urban centers and sporadically in Cuba, Puerto Rico, and the cities of northern Chile it is [š] [šáto] [múšo], and, in Puerto Rico and on the Colombian coast, often [t̮játo] [mút̮jo].

/m/: [m] *mamá, merma* [mamá] [mérma].

/n/: [n] generally, but [ŋ] before a velar consonant, [ñ] before a palatal, and [m] before a labial (*ganga* [gáŋga] *concha* [kóñča] *un peso* [um péso]). /n/ word final before a pause or a vowel tends to be [ŋ] in the Caribbean, southeastern Mexico, Central America, Venezuela, except in the Andean region, coastal Colombia and Ecuador, and the highlands of Ecuador, Peru, and Bolivia: *andén* [andéŋ], *en amor* [eŋ amór]. In the departments of Cauca and Valle of Colombia, one hears [andém].

/ñ/: [ñ] *niño* [níño], but there is a tendency toward [nínjo] in Yucatán.

/l/: [l] *clavel* [klaᵬél]. Syllable final /l/ is often acoustically equivalent to /r/ in Puerto Rico, the Dominican Republic, Venezuela, coastal Colombia, coastal Ecuador, rural Panama, and much of Chile, with some tendency in the Havana area of Cuba: [klaᵬél] [klaᵬér] [klaᵬét̮].

/l̮/: [l̮] *llamar, ella* [l̮amár] [él̮a]. A separate phoneme in Bolivia, Paraguay, Corrientes and Misiones, Argentina, limited sections of northwestern Argentina, most of Peru, and the northern and southern extremes of Ecuador's highlands; in Santiago del Estero, Argentina, it is [ž] as a phoneme in contrast to /y/, as is the case in the central part of Ecuador's highlands.

/r/: [r] *para, decir, tronco* [pára] [desír] [tróŋko]. Word-final /r/ is frequently [ř] and even more frequently [ɹ̥]. In oratorical style, it often becomes [r̄], and in a few coastal areas it is deleted. The combination [tr] is usually [t̆ř] in Guatemala, Costa Rica, the Eastern Cordillera of Colombia, highland Ecuador and highland Bolivia, and sporadically in Mexico and Peru, Paraguay, interior Argentina, and Chile.

/r̄/: [r̄] *parra, rápido* [pár̄a] [rápiɖo]. In Guatemala, Costa Rica (except the western Guanacaste area and the Pacific coast), the Eastern Cordillera of Colombia, central highland Ecuador, the altiplano of Peru and Bolivia, Paraguay, northern and western Argentina, and Chile it tends to be [ř] or [ɹ̥]. It is common in the New Mexico/Colorado dialect area and in highland Mexico. In much of Puerto Rico, in the eastern peninsula of the Dominican Republic, and infrequently on the northern coast of Colombia, the /r̄/ is [R̥].

AMERICAN SPANISH TERRITORY

United States

Mexico

Cuba

Dominican Republic

Haiti

Puerto Rico

Venezuela

Colombia

Ecuador

Peru

Brazil

Bolivia

Paraguay

Chile

Uruguay

Argentina

Numbered Countries
1 Guatemala
2 Belice
3 Honduras
4 El Salvador
5 Nicaragua
6 Costa Rica
7 Panama
8 Trinidad
9 Guyana
10 Surinam
11 French Guiana

Generally the phoneme /ļ/ has been lost,
with leveling to [y]: *valla* and *vaya* [báya].

||||| Sound is sometimes [i̯]: [bai̯a].

☰ Phonemic distinction between /ļ/ and
/y/: *valla* [báļa], *vaya* [báya].

■ Phonemic distinction between /l/[ž]
and /y/[y]: [báža], [báya].

▨ Leveling to palatal fricative [ž] or [š]:
[báža] (or [báša]).

/r̄/ tends to be [r̥̄] or [ř̥]

/r̄/ tends to be [R̥] (or [R]).

/l/ and /r/ syllable final tend to be acoustically equivalent at times.

/s/ IN AMERICA

American Spanish /s/ is usually of high
resonance, more often dorsoalveolar than
apicodental, and in some areas it tends to
be ungrooved, with a lisping effect.

/s/ tends to be [ŝ] as in most of Spain.

/s/ syllable final tends to be aspirated
or deleted.

Suprasegmental Features

As Karen H. Kvavik points out in her significant appraisals of research and methods in Spanish intonational studies (Kvavik and Olson 1974; Kvavik 1976), intonation is one of the least-understood areas of Spanish phonology. In spite of some seventy-five years of observation and a modicum of investigation, there has been a paucity of basic research, a fact that is reflected in pedagogical application. As she indicates, too, there are few studies that show dialectal differences.

In spite of the very clear delineation of Navarro Tomás (1957), not all who have dealt with the matter have perceived the real meanings of *intensidad, tono,* and *cantidad.* Bolinger (1961), in his discussion of *acento melódico* and *acento de intensidad,* demonstrates that there has been confusion in some studies between pitch and stress and that length, an important feature of German, English, and even Italian, is less of a determining factor in Spanish.

Spanish is very sensitive to stress and its grammatical and semantic functions, and it generally continues the stress of Vulgar Latin. French is very sensitive to pitch and length, but not to stress. Expiratory energy makes a big difference between *límite* and *limité.*

Spanish is also sensitive to intonation (musical tone), which has a function in emphasis as well as a syntactic function. The distinction between declaration and interrogation, for instance, is signaled by intonation pattern, as is even the difference between absolute and relative interrogation. Although higher tone often corresponds to stress, this is not always true. The sentence *¿Ha venido?* has stress on the syllable *ni* and higher tone on *do,* and, to complicate matters further, it has been my experience that, though this question intonation may be "standard," it is avoided by Spanish-speaking people of some areas. Mexicans and Cubans in the same class tease each other on this point.

Spanish syllables are not relatively long or short, and studies show that even final syllables may be longer than stressed ones. Much depends on phonetic environment. However, one must recall that the reduction of unstressed vowels in highland regions of America may be related to the matter of length and its relative insignificance in the Spanish phonological pattern. Boyd-Bowman (1952*b*), Canellada de Zamora and Zamora (1960), and Lope Blanch (1966) have written concerning the *vocales caedizas* of Mexico. Navarro Maraví (1964) has detailed his observations on this in central Peru; Toscano Mateus (1953, 1964) has recorded the phenomenon in Ecuador; Albor (1971) has noted it in Nariño, Colombia; and Gordon (1979) has done so in Bolivia. Perhaps it is significant that the vowel reduction is most common in a sibilant environment and in regions where sibilant articulation tends to be tense.

As far as American Spanish dialectology is concerned, most of what has been written about suprasegmental features has to do with intonation. Stress is relatively simple (two levels) and, because of its close tie to grammatical function, seems to be stable and very homogenous in American Spanish.

In Argentina, Fontanella (1966) has dealt with a comparison of two types of regional intonation within her country—that of Tucumán and that of Buenos Aires—and especially with the phenomenon of *glisando*.

Haden and Matluck (1973) have described rather well the intonation of Havana, Cuba, as a part of their analysis of its *habla culta*.

Matluck (1951,1965), who has devoted much time and effort to the analysis of Spanish intonation, describes Mexican intonation and the typical "circumflex" finality that outsiders, including Spanish-speakers, enjoy so much, which seems to be attitudinal—a "man-about-town" style that can be turned on and off—and which may well involve length. Delattre, Olson, and Poenack (1962) have produced an excellent comparison of American English and Mexican Spanish intonations, using as their Mexican subject the painter Diego Rivera. Very evident in the comparison is the gliding quality of English and the angular nature of Spanish.

Lacayo (1962) demonstrates how different the intonation of Nicaragua is from the "standard."

Kvavik (1976) reports on an analysis she conducted, using a melodic analyzer, at the University of Toronto. She compared the intonational patterns of four Spaniards and four Mexicans, and the results show clearly why the Spanish of Spain (except the South) is often referred to as *grave* and that of Mexico as *agudo,* especially in the relation of normal tone to level finality.

There have been other studies, but much is to be done before any picture of dialectal differences can be presented.

Country-by-Country Analysis

In the following country-by-country depictions of phonological traits of American Spanish, I will attempt to show first of all general national features, then regional features within the entity, and finally attitudinal differences that apparently are associated with societal parameters such as age, sex, occupational affiliation, and education—differences that may be referred to as sociolinguistic. The descriptions and accompanying maps are given in the full knowledge that with present information they can only be general, but they do represent progress in ongoing investigation. Linguistic atlases of the Spanish-speaking areas of America do not yet exist, although the Colombian *Atlas lingüístico etnográfico de Colombia (ALEC)* is well on its way to completion. The maps that accompany the statements concerning the Spanish of each country attempt to show variations in pronunciation according to available information, and the overlapped hatchings depict the fact that no clear boundaries may exist, or at least that there are not enough data at this time.

It should be kept in mind, too, that Spanish acculturation of America was a "shotgun" event, with widely separated parts of America receiving the same phases and units of Spanish culture, including language, at the same time. Thus it is that traits of Argentine Spanish are to be found in Central America (in the realm of syntax, the *voseo*) and that several Mexican phenomena are also Bolivian.

Several factors enter into the creation of the differences encountered within individual countries, of which the principal one, as I have indicated, is accessibility to trends in the evolution of Andalusian Castilian. But one must also consider migration from other colonies during the colonial period, the influence of Indian languages, rural-urban dichotomies, and the influence of modern social mobility.

The direction settlers came from proves very important in the consideration of present differences in the Spanish of Argentina, Bolivia, and New Mexico, for instance, and the same could be said for the differences between southern New Mexico and northern New Mexico. As one illustration, the highlands of Bolivia were settled from Peru as we know it today, whereas the llanos people came in from Argentina and Paraguay.

In discussing dialectal differences of the individual countries, I will refer in some cases to centers of linguistic research that may have contributed to Spanish American dialectology.

Argentina

The Spanish of the vast territory of Argentina is of two main types, according to the direction from which the settlers came. Most of the West and Northwest was settled from Peru and Chile late in the sixteenth century or during the early seventeenth century. The Buenos Aires area was settled first about 1535, but after defensive incursions into what is now Paraguay, the *pobladores* returned to Buenos Aires in 1580, and the Humid Pampa was settled gradually from Buenos Aires. Most of these people had come directly from Spain and became identified as *porteños,* while those of the interior who had come in from Peru were *cuyanos.* It is to be noted that Uruguay shares most of the *porteño* traits. As might be expected, the interior of Argentina generally shows more conservative features, in terms of the history of Spanish, than the *porteño* area. The latter, on the main trade routes, received changes that were occurring in the Andalusian dialect of Castilian.

The general impression is that the *argentino* aspirates the /s/ syllable final, but in sections of the Northwest, in Santiago del Estero, the -/s/ is a sibilant. Because /x/ in Argentina is velar rather than laryngeal, the aspiration of -/s/ is not, strictly speaking, an aspiration in every case but a velar fricative, notably before a velar consonant ([búxka]), in variation with a palatal fricative or an aspiration, depending on the environment of the -/s/. Donni de Mirande (1968) shows that, in Rosario and Santa Fe and to the east of the Paraná in Entre Ríos, the /s/ syllable final is not only aspirated but often deleted.

Argentina has one of the most interesting situations in all of Spanish America in the matter of /ʎ/-/y/ distinction and leveling. The impression abroad is that there is one Argentine phoneme, /ž/, but the situation is much more complicated. In Santiago del Estero a phonemic distinction is made, but phonetically it is [ž] and [y]. In Corrientes, Misiones, and the parts of Formosa and Chaco that border on Paraguay, as well as in places on the Bolivian border and in sections of western Argentina near the Andes, the distinction exists in the traditional phonetic manifestations, [ʎ] and [y]. In the *porteño* area and south through Patagonia and east of a line running roughly from Córdoba to Bariloche on the border of Chile, there is leveling to one phoneme whose phonetic form is [ž] and occasionally [š], the latter manifestation becoming more common recently, especially in the speech of women. One now hears the [ž] even in cities of the Northwest—Tucumán, Salta, and Jujuy—and apparently it is gaining ground with population movements westward.

Probably the most convenient way to indicate the original directions of occupation and settlement is to depict the pronunciation of /r̄/. The Buenos Aires area and southern regions settled from there have [r̄], whereas the interior and the North show [řÌ], as is the case in neighboring Chile, Paraguay, and highland Bolivia.

Several sociolinguistic studies have been made in recent years of what might be termed attitudinal phenomena within the phonology of Argentine Spanish. Fontanella de Weinberg (1974a) has demonstrated that men "aspirate" their syllable final /s/ more than women and that, on the basis of occupation, the lowest economic group aspirates the -/s/ at least twice as much as the top group of professional people. Donni de Mirande (1974) has made *encuestas* in Rosario to determine the treatment of the *combinaciones cultas,* and she finds that these consonantal clusters are treated in a much more academic way by the "upper crust" than by the lower groups.

Both Fontanella (1966) and Donni de Mirande (1974) deal with aspects of Argentine intonation (see p. 00). Fontanella compares that of Tucuman with that of Buenos Aires and later describes that of Cordoba, and Donni de Mirande briefly describes that of Rosario.

Important Sources of Information on the
Phonology of Argentine Spanish
(full references in main bibliography)

Special Bibliographies

Davis, Jack Emory. 1966, 1968, 1971a,b. The Spanish of Argentina and Uruguay: An annotated bibliography for 1940–1965 (in six parts).

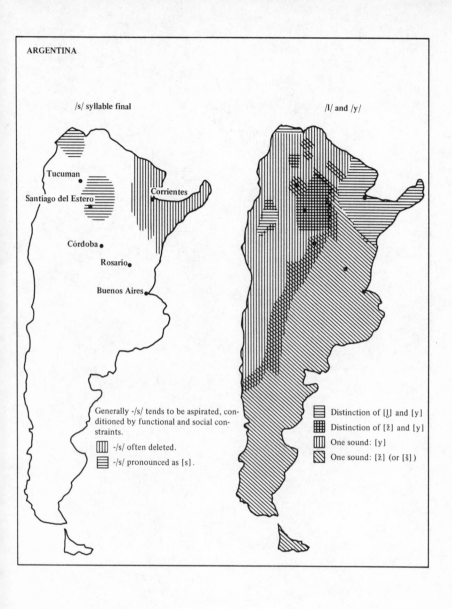

ARGENTINA

/s/ syllable final

/l/ and /y/

Tucuman

Santiago del Estero

Corrientes

Córdoba

Rosario

Buenos Aires

Generally -/s/ tends to be aspirated, conditioned by functional and social constraints.

▥ -/s/ often deleted.

☰ -/s/ pronounced as [s].

☰ Distinction of [ļ] and [y]

▦ Distinction of [ž] and [y]

▥ One sound: [y]

▨ One sound: [ž] (or [š])

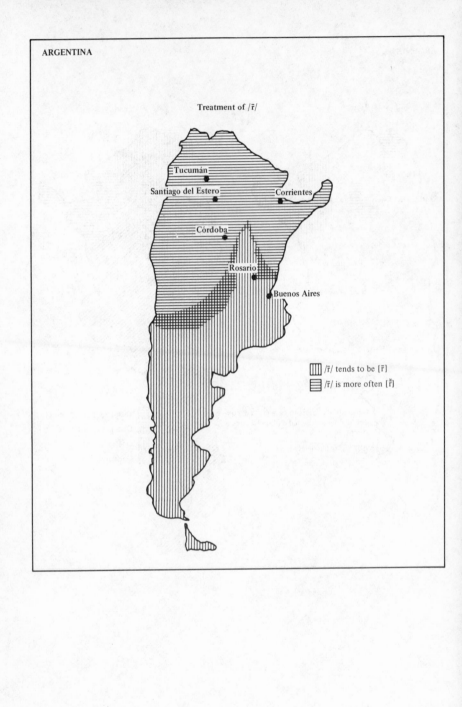

Books and Articles

Vidal de Battini, Berta E. 1949. *El habla rural de San Luis.*

Malmberg, Bertil. 1950. *Etudes sur la phonétique de l'espagnol parlé en Argentine.*

Guitarte, Guillermo. 1955. El ensordecimiento del žeísmo porteño.

Lagmanovich, David. 1957. Sobre el español de Santiago del Estero.

Vidal de Battini, Berta E. 1964*a. El español de la Argentina.*

Honsa, Vladimir. 1965. The phonemic system of Argentinian Spanish.

Fontanella, María B. 1966. Comparación de dos entonaciones regionales argentinas.

———. 1967. La "s" postapical bonaerense.

Donni de Mirande, Nélida. 1967. Recursos afectivos en el habla de Rosario.

———. 1968. El español hablado en Rosario.

———. 1972. Diferencias internas en el español del sur del litoral argentino.

Fontanella de Weinberg, María B. 1973. El rehilamiento bonaerense a fines del siglo XVIII.

———. 1974*a.* Aspectos sociolingüísticos del uso de -s en el español bonaerense.

———. 1974*b.* Comportamiento ante -s de hablantes femeninos y masculinos del español bonaerense.

Donni de Mirande, Nélida. 1974. Grupos consonánticos en Rosario.

Lagmanovich, David. 1976. La pronunciación del español en Tucumán, Argentina, a través de algunos textos dialectales.

Wolf, C. y E. Jiménez. 1977. El yeísmo porteño.

Bolivia

This country, once Alto Peru, was settled by Spanish colonists from two directions, the high altiplano from Peru, the llanos from Paraguay and Argentina. As a result, Bolivia has two principal manifestations of Andalusian Spanish, a very early type in the highlands and a later type that includes changes brought from the *Metrópoli* via the main trade route to Buenos Aires during the late colonial period.

Rather thorough recent investigation (Gordon 1979) has shown convincingly that one feature of Bolivian phonology is common to the whole country in spite of late Andalusian influence in other things. There is a distinction between the two phonemes /ʎ/ and /y/ in all of Bolivia, and the phonetic values are the traditional ones, [ʎ] and [y]. Bolivians make a distinction between *valla* [báʎa] and *vaya* [báya], or between *halla* [áʎa] and *haya* [áya].

Aside from retaining this traditional distinction, the highlands still have [s] for the syllable final sibilant, and in the speech of many people from the altiplano the sibilant is apicoalveolar. Gordon (1979) found this to be the case, and I have recordings of several people from La Paz and Potosí that reveal a frequent /s/ like that of central and northern Spain. In the llanos there is a strong tendency to aspirate /s/ syllable final.

As far as /x/ is concerned, Gordon (1979) discovered that 82 percent of his informants pronounced this as [h], the same articulation that the inhabitants of the llanos tend to use for -/s/ and the same one that is heard, especially in rural sections, for the descendent of Latin F (*hediondo, hosco*).

Another altiplano/llanos difference is in the articulation of /r̄/. In the altiplano it is generally [ř], and in the llanos [r̄], and there is considerable polymorphism.

Vowel reduction in the unstressed syllable is as common as in Mex-

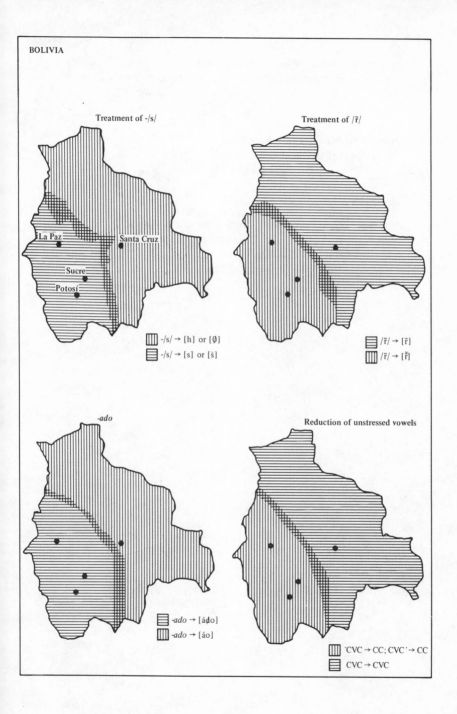

ico and highland Ecuador: *Potsí, ofsina, cochs,* as the tendency might
be represented orthographically, and the termination *-ado* tends to be
[áo] in the llanos.

Important Sources of Information on the
Phonology of Bolivian Spanish
(full references in main bibliography)

Books and Articles

Varas Reyes, Víctor. 1960. *El castellano popular en Tarija.*
Van Wijk, H. L. 1961. Los bolivianismos fonéticos en la obra costum-
    brista de Alfredo Guillén Pinto.
Gordon, Alan M. 1979. Notas sobre la fonética del castellano en Bo-
    livia.

Chile

Traditionally, Chile has been divided linguistically into three sections: North, Central, and South. But with more social mobility and the fast demise of /ʎ/ as a phoneme, few clear-cut geographical distinctions can now be shown. The heavily populated central valley partakes of many of the traits of late Andalusian Spanish through the port of Valparaíso and the city of Santiago, and many of the features that were associated with this region are now to be found in the North and in the South.

Four phenomena seem rather general in Chile: the alveolar rather than palatal articulation of the /č/, [t̠s̠], and the tendency to pronounce /x/ as [ç] before *e, i,* and the /r̄/ as [ř], along with the /tr/ as [t̠ř], as well as the *"costeño"* tendency to aspirate /s/ syllable final.

Most of the country is now *yeísta,* but until about seventy years ago there was evidently a phonemic distinction between /ʎ/ and /y/ in both the North and the South. Oroz (1966) indicates that there are only a few areas south of Santiago (see fig. 9) that preserve /ʎ/ as a separate phoneme.

Oroz (1966) demonstrates that there is a strong tendency to make /l/ and /r/ syllable final acoustically equivalent in much of the nation. In my experience, this tendency seems to be more common in elements of the lower economic groups and especially in the central valley.

There is an interesting trend in some northern towns that may be attitudinal, but since it is also becoming very popular in Panama and to an extent in Cuba and Puerto Rico, it may indicate future development similar to the one that occurred in French in the thirteenth century: the loss of the occlusive element in /č/, which is then heard as [š]. As has been noted (see Preface), speakers may consider the simple sibilant "más suave."

31

Zapata Arellano (1975) indicates that the phoneme /f/ is expressed as [ɸ] much more often than as [f], especially in the countryside.

Important Sources of Information on the
Phonology of Chilean Spanish
(full references in main bibliography)

Books and Articles

Alonso, Amado. 1939. Examen de la teoría indigenista de Rodolfo Lenz.
Rabanales, Ambrosio. 1960. Hiato y antihiato en el español vulgar de Chile.
Oroz, Rodolfo. 1964. *El español de Chile.*
———. 1966. *La lengua castellana en Chile.*
Zapata Arellano, Rodrigo. 1975. Nota sobre la articulación del fonema /f/ en el español de Chile.

CHILE

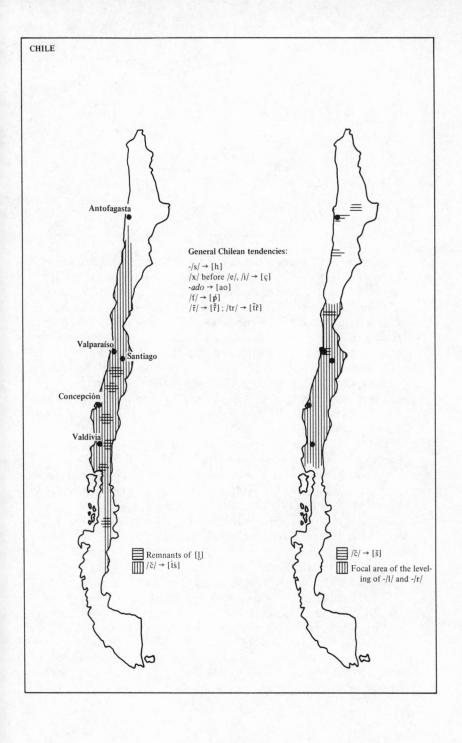

Antofagasta

General Chilean tendencies:

-/s/ → [h]
/x/ before /e/, /i/ → [ç]
-*ado* → [ao]
/f/ → [ɸ]
/r̄/ → [r̄̌] ; /tr/ → [t̆r̆]

Valparaíso
Santiago
Concepción
Valdivia

⊟ Remnants of [ḷ]
▥ /č/ → [ṫš]

⊟ /č/ → [š]
▦ Focal area of the leveling of -/l/ and -/r/

Colombia

With three high mountain ranges and several important cities, Colombia itself might serve as an example of the variegated development of American Spanish from peninsular models. The relative inaccessibility of its high sierras and valleys during the colonial period makes it possible to find at least five manifestations of Andalusian Castilian in this former viceroyalty of Nueva Granada. These dialects represent for the most part stages in the evolution of the language between 1500 and 1800.

It is quite appropriate, then, that Colombians have been concerned and very busy with the study and description of the dialectal differences within the country and with a project that will eventually produce a linguistic atlas.

Plans for a linguistic atlas were made about 1955, and, under the direction of Luis Flórez, Instituto Caro y Cuervo, *encuestas* in the Department of Cundinamarca began about a year later. Flórez (1964) describes the project and the work that had been done at that time, and the monthly *Noticias Culturales* of the Instituto give in detail the accounts of the surveys that were made during the past eight years. Many *investigadores* have taken part in the *encuestas,* often under rather trying conditions. One notes the publication of many "spin-offs" that use data gathered in the process, notably books and articles by José Joaquín Montes Giraldo, Germán de Granda, and Luis Flórez himself. By 1973 about half of Colombia had been mapped phonologically, syntactically, and lexically, and the work must be nearing completion. It was my privilege to teach at the Instituto for several months during the early stages of the project.

The Spanish of Colombia has two general traits in common with that of El Salvador, Honduras, and Nicaragua: the *jota* (/x/) is [h] in all regions, and /b, d, g/ are occlusive after any consonant or after a

34

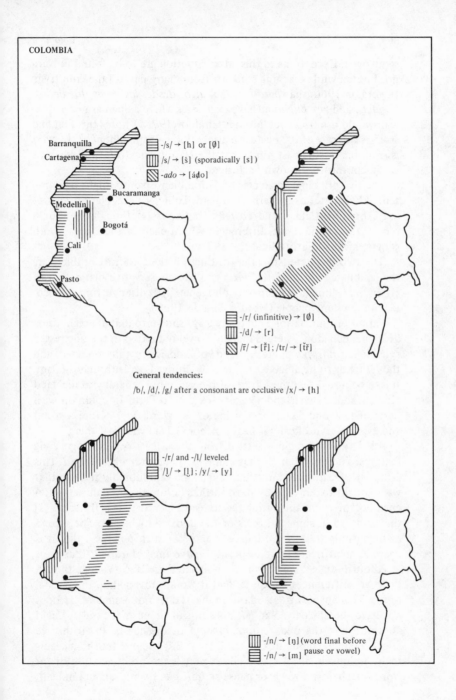

COLOMBIA

Barranquilla
Cartagena
Medellín
Cali
Pasto
Bucaramanga
Bogotá

-/s/ → [h] or [∅]
/s/ → [ṡ] (sporadically [s])
-ado → [áɗo]

-/r/ (infinitive) → [∅]
-/d/ → [r]
/r̄/ → [ř̃] ; /tr/ → [tř̃]

General tendencies:
/b/, /d/, /g/ after a consonant are occlusive /x/ → [h]

-/r/ and -/l/ leveled
/l̯/ → [l̯] ; /y/ → [y]

-/n/ → [ŋ] (word final before
-/n/ → [m] pause or vowel)

semivowel. Exceptions to this latter situation are to be found in Nariño. I noted while teaching students from many parts of the country in Bogotá, in 1960, that *pardo, barba, algo, desde, las vacas, los dados, la ganas,* and *rey bueno* all have occlusives where a Spaniard or a Mexican would use fricatives. Montes Giraldo (1975*a*) notes this fact and stresses the case of the occlusive after a semivowel. Albor (1971), who is from the north coast, finds that the Nariño fricatives in these cases are in contrast to his own occlusives.

The five principal "dialects" of Colombian Spanish might be represented by the terms Eastern Cordillera, Tolima-Cauca, Nariño (*pastuso*), Antioquia-Caldas, and *costeño* (both coasts), though one should recognize that there are differences within each of these areas, both geographical and attitudinal.

The two characteristics that distinguish the Eastern Cordillera are the assibilated /ř/ (and /tr/, -/r/) and the conservative distinction of /ʎ/ and /y/, though the separate phoneme /ʎ/ is disappearing in Bogotá among young people (Montes Giraldo 1969).

Nariño pronunciation is in many ways similar to that of neighboring highland Ecuador. There is marked vowel reduction in the unstressed syllable (*entons, parts,* etc.), the /d/ of *-ado* is generally retained, and the /s/ tends to be apicodental, tensely grooved, and strongly sibilant. It is to be noted that these traits also correspond generally to highland Mexico and Bolivia, and to some extent to Peru. In common with parts of highland Ecuador, voicing of /s/ word final before a vowel and even intervocalically is heard. Albor (1971) writes of this.

Antioquia and regions settled from there have two distinguishing features. The first is an /s/ that is apicoalveolar in many speakers. This is the [ś] of central and northern Spain and undoubtedly the one that was brought to America by most settlers before the Andalusian inflence became rampant during the sixteenth century. It is the same [ś] that is heard in some speakers of the Bolivian highlands. The second distinguishing trait of Antioquia is a /y/ of such tenseness that it is heard as an affricate intervocalically: *mayo* [máŷo], *caballo* [kaɓáŷo].

A fourth dialect area might be designated as Cauca-Valle, although there are differences within it, and it would not include the coastal towns. This Spanish is "standard" in that it does not assibilate /ř/, does not have the apicoalveolar /s/, does not distinguish /l/ and /y/, and does not have the weak *consonantismo* of the coasts. In all this we might include Tolima in this same area. But the one trait that seems to be unique in the Cauca-Valle region is the pronunciation of /n/ word final before a vowel or pause as /m/: *pan* [pam]; *andén* [andém].

This became quite evident to me while I was giving talks at the university in Cali, but the matter needs further study.

Coastal Colombian Spanish is similar in most respects to that of the Caribbean: the aspiration or loss of -/s/, velar /n/ in open transition (*en amor*), the leveling of -/l/ and -/r/ in some sections, and the articulation of /č/ as [ťj]. As a part of the *ALEC* project, several *encuestas* on the north coast of Colombia were made under the direction of Luis Flórez (1964), and in more recent times the Pacific coast has received attention. Montes Giraldo (1974, 1975*b*) has done considerable work there, as has Germán de Granda (1973, 1977). Differences between the Atlantic and Pacific coasts have been noted in the articulation of intervocalic /d/, which is often heard as [r] on the Pacific side, and intervocalic /k/, which at times is a glottal stop on the Pacific side. Although the picture is incomplete, there appear to be differences between North and South on the Pacific side.

Important Sources of Information on the Phonology of Colombian Spanish

(full references in main bibliography)

Books and Articles

Flórez, Luis. 1951*b*. *La pronunciación del español en Bogotá.*
———. 1957. *Habla y cultura en Antioquia.*
Montes Giraldo, José J. 1959. Del español hablado en Bolívar, Colombia.
Flórez, Luis. 1964. El español hablado en Colombia y su atlas lingüístico.
———. 1965. *El español hablado en Santander.*
Montes Giraldo, José J. 1967. El atlas lingüístico etnográfico de Colombia (ALEC): Encuestas, exploradores, publicaciones, 1956–1966.
Flórez, Luis. 1969. *El español hablado en el Departamento del Norte de Santander.*
Cock Hincapié, Olga. 1969. *El seseo en el Nuevo Reino de Granada: 1550–1650.*
Montes Giraldo, José J. 1969. ¿Desaparece la "ll" de la pronunciación bogotana?
———. 1970. *Dialectología y geografía lingüística: Notas de orientación.*

Albor, Hugo. 1971. Observaciones sobre la fonología del español hablado en Nariño.

Granda, Germán de. 1973. Dialectología, historia social y sociología lingüística en Iscuande, Depto. de Nariño, Colombia.

Montes Giraldo, José J. 1974. El habla del Chocó.

——. 1975a. Breves notas de fonética actual del español.

Granda, Germán de. 1977. *Estudios sobre un área dialectal hispanoamericana de población negra: Las tierras bajas occidentales de Colombia.*

Flórez, Luis. 1978. Sobre algunas formas de pronunciar muchos colombianos el español: Datos y problemas.

Noticias Culturales (Instituto Caro y Cuervo), monthly since 1966, has many accounts of the *encuestas* for the *ALEC.*

Costa Rica

As Arturo Agüero (1964) indicates, the territory of the first settlements in this area was known as Nueva Cartago, but before the end of
the sixteenth century Costa Rica was becoming the usual term. As a
part of the Audiencia de Guatemala, definite settlements date from
1561, mainly in what is now called the Valle Central, and the *pobladores* were largely people who had already lived in other colonies:
Mexico, Guatemala, and Nicaragua. It is interesting that the phonology
of Costa Rican Spanish resembles that of Guatemala more than that
of any other region. It was not until 1824, shortly after independence,
that the Nicaraguan province of Guanacaste voluntarily annexed itself
to Costa Rica, and today the two types of pronunciation are that of
the central valley and that of Guanacaste and the adjacent area of
Puntarenas. History shows that the *ticos* (from the habitual dissimila-
tion of diminutives with a preceding /t/: *momentico,* also common in
Colombia and Cuba) of the highlands had little communication with
the outside until recent times.

Like Guatemala, Costa Rica is noted for the assibilation of /r̄/, /tr/,
and -/r/, except in Guanacaste and on the Pacific coast. In common
with residents of all Central American and Caribbean countries, Costa
Ricans pronounce /n/ word final before a pause or vowel as [ŋ]: [eŋ
amór], but [enamorár]. As in the other Central American countries
(not Panama), intervocalic /y/ (there is no /ʎ/) weakens to the point
of elimination through vocalization, and in Guanacaste, as in Nicaragua, Honduras, and El Salvador, there is considerable hypercorrection
of this tendency.

Quite a contrast is found in the matter of -/s/. While San José, He-
redia, Cartago, and territories settled from the central valley articulate
a clear sibilant, in Guanacaste, and to some extent on the whole Pacific coast, -/s/ tends to be aspirated.

39

In recent decades, English-speaking people from the Caribbean have settled on the Caribbean side of Costa Rica, Nicaragua, and Honduras. Puerto Limón, Bluefields, and Puerto Cabezas are examples of places where much English is heard.

Important Sources of Information on the
Phonology of Costa Rican Spanish
(full references in main bibliography)

Articles

Chavarría-Aguilar, O. L. 1951. The phonemes of Costa Rican Spanish.
Agüero, Arturo. 1964. El español de Costa Rica y su atlas lingüístico.
Wilson, Jack Leroy. 1971. A generative phonological study of Costa Rican Spanish.
Berk-Seligman, Susan, and Seligman, Mitchell A. 1978. The phonological correlates of social stratification in the Spanish of Costa Rica.

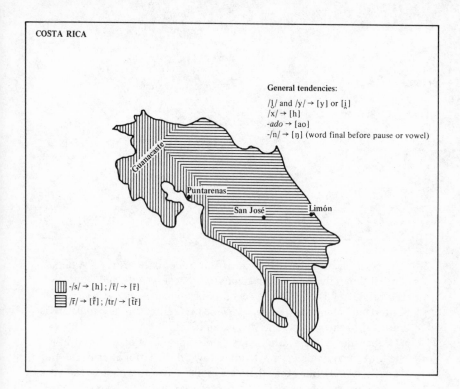

COSTA RICA

General tendencies:

/ļ/ and /y/ → [y] or [i̯]
/x/ → [h]
-*ado* → [ao]
-/n/ → [ŋ] (word final before pause or vowel)

Guanacaste

Puntarenas

San José   Limón

-/s/ → [h] ; /r̄/ → [řr̄]
/r̄/ → [řr̄] ; /tr/ → [třr̄]

Cuba

The Spanish of Cuba is typical of the trade-route areas of America, since it shows the Andalusian trends of the seventeenth and eighteenth centuries, trends that do not seem to have reached the less accessible hinterland. Menéndez Pidal (1957–58) refers to this as *comerical* as opposed to the viceregal of Mexico and Peru.

Cubans tend to aspirate their syllable final /s/ or drop it altogether, the lower economic classes tending toward the latter alternative. But Terrell (1975*a*) finds that there are constraints other than social ones in the deletion of the -/s/. I have correspondence on tape with three members of the same family: a lawyer, an actor, and a housewife. The actor pronounced all his sibilants and even gave apicoalveolar articulation to some; the lawyer aspirated about half his syllable-final sibilants; and the housewife, who spoke very rapidly by comparison, aspirated or deleted most.

Word-final /n/ is normally [ŋ] before a pause or a vowel, but Terrell (1975*b*) finds that in some cases there is no consonant, but simply nasalization of the preceding vowel, and that Puerto Ricans and Panamanians nasalize the vowel even more than Cubans.

Perhaps more than in other area of America, the /r̄/ of Cuba tends to be voiceless, especially among women speakers. The articulation could be represented as [r̥̄].

Many observers have noted that the /č/ is weakening to [š] among Cubans, and here again it seems to be more common among women than men. In two other regions this development is apparently taking place: Panama and northern Chile, especially in the cities.

The acoustical equivalency of -/l/ and -/r/ is to be noted today, especially among *habaneros.* Haden and Matluck (1973) report that it is much less frequent than in other parts of the Caribbean.

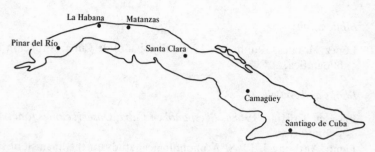

CUBA

La Habana   Matanzas

Pinar del Río

Santa Clara

Camagüey

Santiago de Cuba

General tendencies:

-/s/ → [h] or [∅]
-/n/ → [ŋ] (word final before pause or vowel)

Attitudinal tendencies:

-/r/ → [l] or assimilated to C (*puerta* [pwelta] or [pwetta])
/č/ → [š]
/r̄/ → [r̜̄]

Important Sources of Information on the
Phonology of Cuban Spanish
(full references in main bibliography)

Bibliography

López Morales, Humberto. 1968. El español de Cuba: Situación bibliográfica.

Books and Articles

Ibaseşcu, Cristina. 1968*a*. *El español en Cuba: Observaciones fonéticas
y fonológicas.*
Lamb, Anthony J. 1968. A phonological study of the Spanish of Havana, Cuba.
Vallejo-Claros, Bernardo. 1970. La distribución y estratificación de
/r/ /r̄/ /s/ en el español cubano.
Haden, Ernest F., and Matluck, Joseph. 1973. El habla culta de la Habana: Análisis fonológico preliminar.
Terrell, Tracy D. 1975*a*. Functional constraints on deletion of word
final /s/ in Cuban Spanish.
———. 1975*b*. La nasal implosiva y final en el español de Cuba.
Guitart, Jorge Miguel. 1976. *Markedness and a Cuban dialect of Spanish.*
Costa Sánchez, Manuel. 1977*a*. Análisis acústico-articulatorio de las
cinco vocales del español hablado en Cuba.
———. 1977*b*. Descripción de particularidades acústico-articulatorias
de algunos sonidos consonánticos del español hablado en Cuba.
Terrell, Tracy D. 1977*a*. La aspiración y elisión en el español cubano.
Corrientes actuales en la dialectología del Caribe hispánico. 1978.
Guitart, Jorge M. 1978. A propósito del español de Cuba y Puerto
Rico: Hacia un modelo sociolingüístico de la sociodialectal.
Hammond, Robert M. 1978. An experimental verification of the pho-
nemic status of open and closed vowels in Caribbean Spanish.

The Dominican Republic

Recent studies by Jorge Morel (1974) and Jiménez Sabater (1975) have given us a clearer picture of the Dominican dialect of Spanish than the general studies of Henríquez Ureña (1940) and Navarro Tomás (1956), and, though the dialect is part of a general Caribbean type, there are regional and certainly attitudinal differences, from group to group within the regions.

Tendencies that seem common to the whole country are the aspiration or deletion of /s/ syllable final, and there must be attitudinal nuances based on societal parameters, the articulation of /x/ as [h], and the word-final /n/ before a pause or vowel as [ŋ]. In the area of /ʎ/-/y/, there is, of course, one phoneme, /y/.

Since the articulation of -/r/ in most sections of the Dominican Republic is not a clear vibrant, it becomes acoustically so close to /l/ when syllable final that it is difficult to distinguish. In some areas the solution seems to be a "doubling" of the final consonant in the preconsonantal position, and in others a semivowel takes the place of the /r/ or /l/. In the Southwest the tendency is apparently the most conservative: *carne* [kárne] ; in the North generally, it is [káine] ; near the capital, Santo Domingo, it tends to be [kálne], and in the peninsula of the Southeast the doubling occurs, [kánne]. But it stands to reason that the distinctions are not always so neatly drawn.

The /r̄/ is generally a trill, with a strong trend toward the voiceless variety [r̥̄], as in Cuba. In the extreme Southeast the /r̄/ is usually [R̥]: *tierra* [tjéR̥a], *Ramón* [R̥amóŋ].

**Important Sources of Information on the
Phonology of Dominican Spanish**
(full references in main bibliography)

Books and Articles

Henríquez Ureña, Pedro. 1940. *El español en Santo Domingo.*
Navarro Tomás, Tomás. 1956. Apuntes sobre el español dominicano.
Jorge Morel, Elercia. 1974. Estudio lingüístico de Santo Domingo:
Aportación a la geografía lingüística del Caribe e Hispano América.
Jiménez Sabater, Maximiliano A. 1975. Más datos sobre el español de
la República Dominicana.
———. 1977. Estructuras morfosintácticas en el español dominicano:
Corrientes actuales en la dialectología del Caribe hispánico. 1978.

THE DOMINICAN REPUBLIC

General tendencies:

/x/ → [h]
-/s/ → [h] or [∅]
-/n/ → [ŋ] (word final
  before vowel or pause)

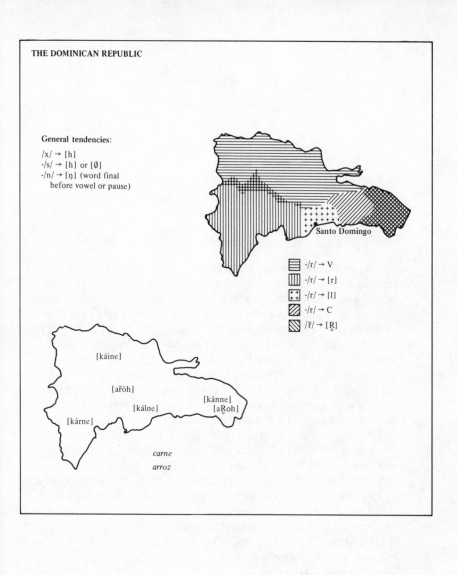

Santo Domingo

☰ -/ɾ/ → V
▥ -/ɾ/ → [ɾ]
⊕ -/ɾ/ → [l]
▨ -/ɾ/ → C
▧ /r̄/ → [R̥]

[káine]

[ar̄óh]

[kálne]

[kánne]
[aR̥oh]

[kárne]

carne
arroz

Ecuador

Ecuatorianos customarily divide their territory into Costa, Sierra Interandina, and Oriente, but linguistically it is a little more complicated. The big dichotomy phonologically today is the Costa/Sierra one, owing principally, no doubt, to the inaccessibility of the towns of the Sierra during the colonial period to phases of the evolution of Andalusian Castilian, but the Sierra itself has a central core extending roughly from north of Quito southward to Cuenca that shows at least three traits that are not present in the more traditional speech of Carchi in the North and Loja in the South. The coast has the usual features of *costeño* Spanish, and Oriente, settled mostly from the Sierra, has the phonology of the region of its settlers.

All *serranos* seem to pronounce /s/ with deliberate tenseness: [s], much as is the case in Mexico and Bolivia and Peru. Like highland Mexicans and Bolivians of the altiplano, and Peruvians to an extent, they often slight the vowel of pretonic and posttonic syllables, especially in a sibilant environment: *of(i)cina, accident(e)s, pas(e) (u)sted*.

In the central core of Ecuador, from north of Quito to far south of Ambato, a distinction is made between the phonemes /ļ/ and /y/, but as [ž] and [y] respectively: *valla* [báža], *vaya* [báya]; /r̃/ tends to be [ř̃], and, almost uniquely in America, -/s/ word final before a vowel is [z] (*las aguas* [laz áǵwas]).

One might designate a second highland dialect, divided by the central area just referred to. This would include the province of Carchi on the Colombian border as well as the southern provinces of Azuay, Loja, Zamora, part of El Oro, and, for some features, Cañar. Regions of Oriente settled from these would be included in this type of highland Spanish. In these areas, including Cañar, the phonemes /ļ/ and /y/ are [ļ] and [y], and, judging from my experience with *quiteño* students who try to make this particular distinction when reading but

48

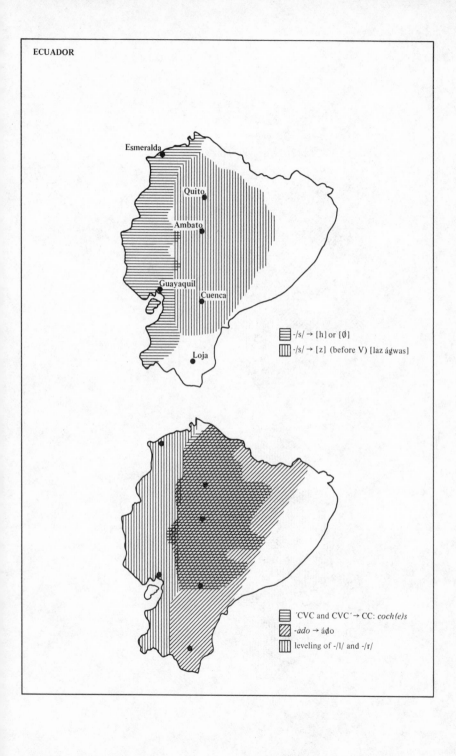

ECUADOR

-/s/ → [h] or [∅]
-/s/ → [z] (before V) [laz ágwas]

´CVC and CVC´ → CC: coch(e)s
-ado → áđo
leveling of -/l/ and -/r/

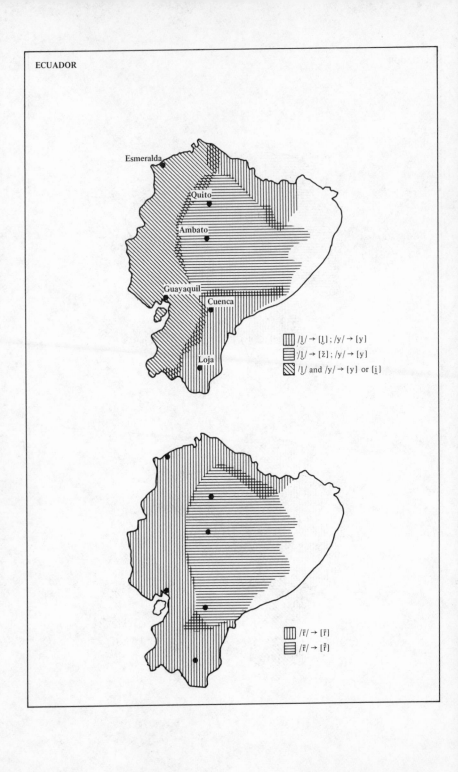

ECUADOR

Esmeralda

Quito

Ambato

Guayaquil

Cuenca

Loja

/ḷ/ → [ḷ] ; /y/ → [y]
/ḷ/ → [ž] ; /y/ → [y]
/ḷ/ and /y/ → [y] or [i̯]

/ř̄/ → [r̄]
/ř̄/ → [ř̄]

who naturally pronounce [ž] and [y], this is the prestige mode of the country. In the extreme North and South, /r̄/ is [ř], but this does not include Cañar. In Carchi, Loja, and El Oro, *las aguas* is [las áǥwas].

As I have indicated, the port of Guayaquil and the lowlands in general have *costeño* phonology that reminds one of Cuba. The /s/ syllable final is aspirated or deleted, the /r/ is a trill [r̄], the termination *-ado* is usually [ao] or [aw], the -/l/ and -/r̄/ tend to be acoustically equivalent, and it is difficult to distinguish *harto* from *alto*.

Important Sources of Information on the Phonology of Ecuadorian Spanish
(full references in main bibliography)

Books and Articles

Boyd-Bowman, Peter. 1953. Sobre la pronunciación del español en el Ecuador.

King, Harold V. 1953. Sketch of Guayaquil Spanish phonology.

Toscano Mateus, Humberto. 1953. *El español en el Ecuador.*

———. 1964. El español hablado en el Ecuador.

El Salvador

This little country, along with Honduras and Nicaragua, represents a phonology that lies between the highland conservatism of Mexico, Colombia, and the Andes and the lowland "relaxed" trends of much of coastal Spanish America.

It was my privilege to be a research consultant in dialectology at the Instituto Tropical de Investigaciones Científicas in San Salvador in the summer of 1952, after another summer of fieldwork in El Salvador, sponsored in part by an American University. During the same period, Professor Heberto Lacayo of Florida State University was interviewing informants in his native Nicaragua.

One of our "discoveries" during these investigations was the occlusive articulation of /b, d, g/ after any consonant or semivowel. Although Professor Lacayo was a native of Nicaragua, he had lived abroad for some time and had not realized that this was a constant in the speech of that area. To me, accustomed to the "standard" mode of Mexico and Spain, the effect was staccato. Such pronunciations as these were heard: *desde el verde jardín* [déḥde el β́érde hardíŋ] instead of [dézɟe el β́érɟe xarɟín]; [laḥ bárbah del r̄ej de β́ahtos]; [margaríta a ɟíčo álgo]. Although there is much polymorphism in other features of the Spanish of the area, this trait was almost 100 percent constant. In a word like *deuda,* for instance, the phonetic rendition was [déwda], [débda], [dekda], [degda], and so on, but always [d].

Although the foregoing might be considered a conservative feature in the evolution of Spanish from Latin, El Salvador has many of the characteristics of *costeño* Spanish. The *jota* is a weak [h] and tends to drop intervocalically in emphatic expressions: [méiko] [pendéo] (*pendejo*), with lengthening of the preceding vowel at times. The /s/ syllable final is frequently aspirated, and in many speakers the articu-

EL SALVADOR

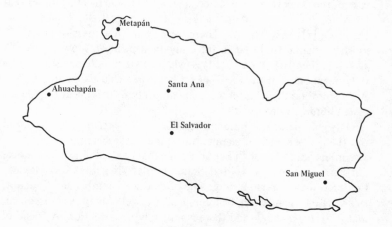

General tendencies:

/b, d, g/ → [b, d, g] (after another consonant or semivowel)
-/n/ → [ŋ] (word final before pause or vowel)
-/l/- and -/y/- → [y] or [i̯]; and *ía* → [íya] (*día* → [díya])
/s/ → [s], [θ]
/r̄/ → [r̄]
/x/ → [h]

Attitudinal traits:

-/s/ → [s], [h], [θ] ([z] or [ḥ] before voiced consonant)
/f/ → [ɸ] or [f]

Hypercorrection of *combinaciones cultas*:

nn, nm, mn, gn, gm → [ŋn] or [ŋm]
(*innumerable, inmediato, columna, ignorante, enigma*)
pt, bs, ps → [kt], [ks], [ks] (*acepto, absoluto, Concepción*)

lation of /s/ approaches [θ] but lacks the tenseness of that of Spain. The impression is that of a lisp, and the tongue is flat and ungrooved. Many speakers still show a proclivity to assimilate regressively in the case of the /s/ before a voiced consonant. Canfield (1960a) found that *las vacas, los gatos,* and *los dedos* elicited several allophones of /s/: [ḥ], [h], [s], [z], [θ̬], [z̧]. There were even a few cases of initial /s/: as [h]: [hánta ána]. /s/ in the truly final position most frequently gave [s], then [h], then [θ]. It is evident that the sibilant situation is polymorphous, but the /b, d, g/ set kept the occlusive nature. Out of 212 recordings of /d/ after a consonant, only 8 (from near the Guatemalan border) were fricative.

Only one person, a resident of an *asilo de ancianos,* pronounced the /ʎ/ as a separate phoneme, but it may have been an affectation. The intervocalic /y/ of El Salvador, like that of all of Central America, northern Mexico, the United States border area, the New Mexico/ Colorado dialect region, and some of coastal Colombia and Ecuador, lacks tenseness and often becomes a semivowel or may even disappear: *silla* [sía], *bella* [béa], and there is much hypercorrection. A friend of mine used to begin a discussion with: *Vea usted, amigo* [béya usté amíǥo].

Among the *combinaciones cultas,* there are some interesting solutions to problems that apparently had been solved in the time of Cervantes. [k] and [ŋ] are often present in dealing with these: *Concepción* [konseksjóŋ]; *concepto* [konsékto]; *himno* [íŋno]; *innecesario* [iŋnesesárjo]; *ignorante* [iŋnorante]. Interesting hypercorrections are heard: *piscina* [piksína]; *automóbil* [aktomóƀil]; *estación* [ekstasjóŋ]; *sport* [ekspór].

Important Sources for Information on the
Phonology of Salvadorean Spanish
(full references in main bibliography)

Articles

Canfield, D. Lincoln. 1953a. Andalucismos en la pronunciación salvadoreña.
———. 1960a. Observaciones sobre el español salvadoreño.

Guatemala

The phonology of Guatemalan Spanish resembles that of Costa Rica more than that of neighboring El Salvador. It will be recalled that during the days of the colonial Audiencia de Guatemala many of the *pobladores* of Costa Rica had arrived from other established colonies, including Guatemala.

Perhaps the outstanding feature of the phonology of the area to a person from another Spanish-speaking region is the strong assibilation of /r̄/ and of /r/ (except in intervocalic position). Not only is the assibilation quite general, but it is often of a voiceless nature. I recall hearing a maid in a home ask about the [r̊ópa], and my immediate reaction was that she had said *sopa*. The voiceless assibilated /r̄/ is very similar in point of articulation, and acoustically, to the apicoalveolar [ṡ] of Spain. I also recall hearing a youth say in reply to a question about the identity of a group of tents and apparatus: *"Es un circo."* Phonetically it seemed to be [síṡko], in a sense a recapitulation of earlier Spanish sibilant gradation. *Parque* gives the effect of [páṡke], and recordings of two Guatemalan poets give ample evidence of r̥ in the final situation.

The *jota* of Guatemala tends to be [h] rather than [x], although in careful or emphatic speech it may become [x́].

In common with all Central American countries (except Panama), intervocalic /y/ is so weak that it disappears: *capilla* [kapía] or is only a semivowel: *mayo* [má i̯o], and there are tendencies toward hypercorrection.

Guatemalans generally pronounce the /s/ with clarity as a tense, grooved sibilant, as in Mexico (except the Gulf coast) and in the Andes.

While teaching at the Universidad de San Carlos and again with an NDEA institute in Guatemala, I have noted the same tendencies of

55

hypercorrection in the *combinaciones cultas* that is present in El Salvador.

Important Sources of Information on the
Phonology of Guatemalan Spanish
            (full references in main bibliography)

Articles

Predmore, Richard L. 1945. La pronunciación de varias consonantes
    en el español de Guatemala.
Canfield, D. Lincoln. 1951*b*. Guatemalan *rr* and *s:* A recapitulation
    of Old Spanish sibilant gradation.

GUATEMALA

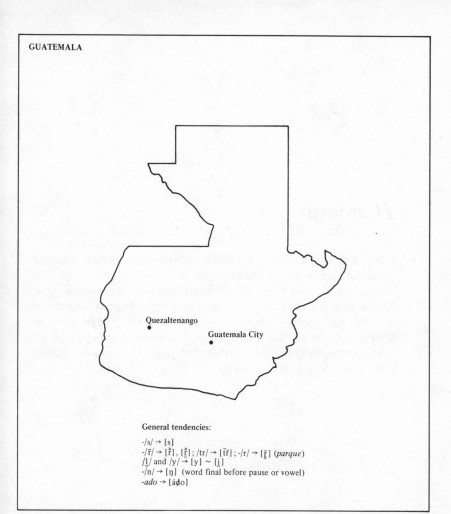

Quezaltenango

Guatemala City

General tendencies:

-/s/ → [s]
-/r̄/ → [ř], [ɹ̌] ; /tr/ → [tř] ; -/r/ → [ɹ̌] (*parque*)
/ʎ/ and /y/ → [y] ~ [i̯]
-/n/ → [ŋ] (word final before pause or vowel)
-*ado* → [áđo]

Honduras

This country, with El Salvador and Nicaragua, seems to form a linguistic unit in many respects, but especially in phonology and syntax. Unfortunately, there is a paucity of information on the phonology of Honduras, though I did make recordings in Tegucigalpa in the summer of 1952. Apparently there is no information on the pronunciation of Spanish in Ceiba and San Pedro Sula and in the interior in general.

My interviews indicated a pattern like that of El Salvador, at least as far as the capital area is concerned.

HONDURAS

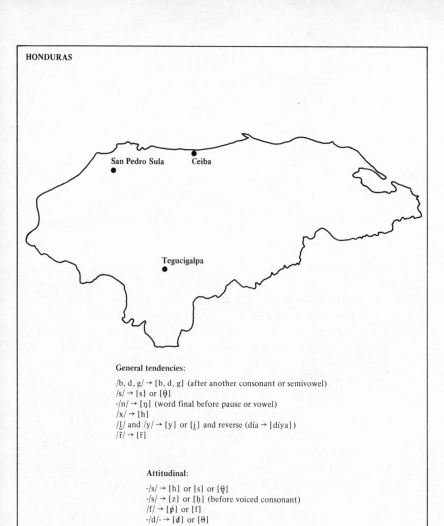

General tendencies:

/b, d, g/ → [b, d, g] (after another consonant or semivowel)
/s/ → [s] or [θ̞]
-/n/ → [ŋ] (word final before pause or vowel)
/x/ → [h]
/l̬/ and /y/ → [y] or [i̬] and reverse (día → [díya])
/r̄/ → [r̄]

Attitudinal:

-/s/ → [h] or [s] or [θ̞]
-/s/ → [z] or [h̬] (before voiced consonant)
/f/ → [ɸ] or [f]
-/d/- → [d̬] or [θ]

Mexico

Among other speakers of Spanish, a Mexican is recognized by his intonation (see section on suprasegmental features, pp. 18–19), by his tendency to lengthen the articulation of /s/, and by a general preference for the consonant over the vowel. But, aside from the intonation, these same traits have been noted in the Andes from southern Colombia through Bolivia, and with further study it may be shown that the intonation of northwestern Argentina is not too different from that of highland Mexico.

An American, Charles Marden (1896), was probably the first to give a fairly reliable description of the phonology of Mexico City Spanish, with some comparisons with certain distinct features of nearby areas. In 1933 Gutiérrez Eskildsen let us know "cómo hablamos en Tabasco." Suárez (1945) described well the Spanish of his native Yucatán, and another American who has been active in American Spanish dialectology, Matluck (1951), gave a detailed account of the pronunciation of the Valley of Mexico. Other *norteamericanos,* Boyd-Bowman (1952*a, b,* 1960), King (1952), and Cárdenas (1955) have contributed to the data on Mexican Spanish phonology.

Since the middle 1960s a great deal of work has been done and is still being done on the analysis of the Spanish of this vast territory, now the largest country of Spanish speech in terms of population. These organized efforts have been conducted under the direction of Juan Lope Blanch of the Colegio de México. *Encuestas* have been conducted in nearly all of Mexico (Lope Blanch 1975), and several spin-offs of these investigations have been published, but descriptions of the Spanish of individual settlements, such as exist for Colombia, have still to come from these efforts. Suffice it to say that, for one who has lived, studied, and taught in Mexico for several years, there are still things to be learned and still some surprises.

Indications are approximate for lack of information)

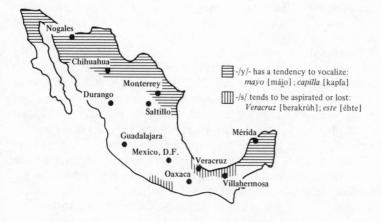

▤ -/y/- has a tendency to vocalize:
mayo [máịo] ; *capilla* [kapfa]

▥ -/s/ tends to be aspirated or lost:
Veracruz [berakrúh]; *este* [éhte]

General tendency in rural areas:
-*ado* [ao] ([merkáo])

General tendency in Southeast:
/x/ → [h] ([méhico], [báha])

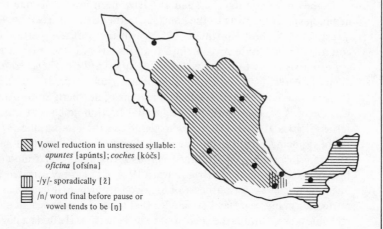

▨ Vowel reduction in unstressed syllable:
apuntes [apúnts]; *coches* [kóčs]
oficina [ofsína]

▥ -/y/- sporadically [ž]

▤ /n/ word final before pause or
vowel tends to be [ŋ]

As Matluck (1963) points out, the vowel /e/ in Mexican Spanish does not follow exactly the pattern of the /e/ of Spain as described by Navarro Tomás (1957), especially in the closed syllable, where in general it tends to be more closed than the peninsular vowel. It seems that reasons for this should be sought in the differences in point of articulation of the following consonants between the Castilian of Spain and that of Mexico.

Vowel reduction in the unstressed syllable, following or preceding primary stress, is very common in highland Mexico, which means most of the nation. Boyd-Bowman (1952*b*) and Lope Blanch (1966) write of this phenomenon, which makes *bloques para apuntes* sound like [blóks pára apúnts]. *Es necesario ir a la oficina* becomes [ez nessárjo ir a la ofsína]. As one who has lived with this habit for many years, I find it difficult to pinpoint the attitude it may reflect, but it seems to indicate impatience with delay, a certain urbanity, and at the same time a familiarity with the listener. The tendency is as common in Bolivia as in Mexico, as Gordon (1979) has indicated, and it is definitely associated with highland Ecuador, Nariño, Colombia, and to some extent with Peru.

The *jota* of Mexico is generally prepalatal or postpalatal, depending on the vocalic environment. In the southern regions of the country and along the Gulf coast, the articulation is rather [h], as is the case in Yucatán. In recordings I have made, the *jota* of Oaxaca wavers between [x̣] and [h]. In the speech of most highland Mexicans, the name of the country itself is [méçiko].

In the entire country, /ļ/ and /y/ have been leveled to one phoneme, in spite of reports to the contrary in the past, reports that were investigated by Boyd-Bowman (1952*b*). In the northern part of the country, from Monterrey northward and westward, the intervocalic /y/ often weakens to a semivowel or disappears: *bella* [béịa], *capilla* [kapía], *mayo* [maịo]. This phenomenon is characteristic of all of Central America and of some coastal regions of northern South America. Records of a /y/ with audible palatal friction go back at least as far as Charles Marden (1896), who described the intervocalic /y/ of Puebla as being similar to the French *j*. *Rehilamiento* is the term used by Spanish-speaking writers since Navarro Tomás for what amounts to a prepalatal voiced fricative. Alvar (1966–67) has investigated the phenomenon in areas southeast of Mexico City, where it had been reported for many years, and concludes that there is a great deal of polymorphism even within the speech of a single person. He finds a degree of *rehilamiento* at times in Santo Tomás de Ajusco, near Mexico, D.F., some in Puebla and Tlaxcala, but more in Oaxaca, where *caballo* may be [kaβážo] .

It has been my observation after many extended visits in Oaxaca that the intervocalic /y/ is only now and then an audible fricative and rarely if ever reaches the point of [ž]. These observations are supported by recordings of youths of the area. In conversations with native teachers I discovered, however, that the /y/ with audible friction is considered "fino hablar."

The /n/ of Mexico varies allophonically in the standard ways, but in southern Mexico and Yucatán it tends to be velar before a pause or an initial vowel in a following word.

The /r̄/ of Mexico has two variants: [r̄] and [ř]. The former is by far the more common. The assibilated variety is heard sporadically in circumstances that seem to me to be those of affectation: reading poetry, in drawing-room conversations *de confianza;* it is heard among women more than among men, and seems to be an attitudinal variant.

Lope Blanch (1975) reports a retroflex /r/, which he transcribes [R] , in several localities of Yucatán, and, though Maya does not have this sound, he raises the question of possible Maya influence.

Important Sources of Information on the Phonology of Mexican Spanish
(full references in main bibliography)

Special Bibliographies

Davis, Jack Emory. 1971*b*. The Spanish of Mexico: An annotated bibliography for 1940–1969.

Books and Articles

Marden, Charles. 1896. *The phonology of the Spanish dialect of Mexico City.*
Suárez, Víctor M. 1945. *El español que se habla en Yucatán: Apuntamientos filológicos.*
Matluck, Joseph. 1951. *La pronunciación en el español del Valle de México.*
Boyd-Bowman, Peter. 1952*b*. La pérdida de vocales átonas en la planicie mexicana.
King, Harold V. 1952. Outline of Mexican Spanish phonology.
Boyd-Bowman, Peter. 1960. *El habla de Guanajuato.*

Canellada de Zamora, Maria J., and Zamora, Alonso V. 1960. Vocales caducas en el español mexicano.

Matluck, Joseph. 1963. La *é* trabada en la ciudad de México.

Lope Blanch, Juan M. 1966. En torno a las vocales caedizas del español mexicano.

Alvar, Manuel. 1966–67. Polimorfismo y otros aspectos fonéticos en el habla de Santo Tomás Ajusco.

Lope Blanch, Juan. 1966–67. Sobre el rehilamiento de ll/y en México.

Cárdenas, Daniel. 1967. El español de Jalisco.

Lope Blanch, Juan. 1967. La -r final del español mexicano y el sustrato nahua.

———. 1969. Para la delimitación de las zonas dialectales de México.

Spyropoulos, Esperanza M. 1969. The phonology of the word in a Spanish dialect.

Lope Blanch, Juan M. 1972. *Estudios sobre el español de México.*

———. 1974. Dialectología mexicana y sociolingüística.

———. 1975. Un caso de posible influencia maya en el español mexicano.

Perissinotto, Giorgio Sabino Antonio. 1975. *Fonología del español hablado en la Ciudad de México: Ensayo de un método sociolingüístico.*

Cavazos Garza, Israel. 1976. El habla del noreste de México: Comentarios.

México. Universidad Nacional. Centro de Lingüística. 1976. *El habla popular de la Ciudad de México.*

Cassano, Paul V. 1977. La influencia maya en la fonología del español de Yucatán.

Estudios sobre el español hablado en las principales ciudades de América. 1977.

Nicaragua

As I have indicated, the phonologies of Nicaragua, Honduras, and El Salvador apparently form a unit in American Spanish. Lacayo (1954, 1962) has given us about the only detailed information on the phonology of Nicaraguan Spanish, much of which is depicted in symbolic terms on the map following, under "general tendencies," "attitudinal traits," and "hypercorrection of *combinaciones cultas.*" If there is any difference between the phonology of Nicaraguan Spanish and that of El Salvador, it is in the articulation of the /s/ syllable final. The *nicaragüense* apparently aspirates this more often than the *salvadoreño*.

The occlusive /b, d, g/ after any consonant or semivowel, the tendency of many to "lisp" the /s/, the weak articulation of intervocalic /y/, the strongly trilled /r̄/, the velar /n/ before pause or a vowel, and the attitudinal polymorphism encountered in -/s/, /f/, and -/d/- are present in both Nicaragua and El Salvador—and in Honduras, as far as we know. The proclivity for [ŋ] in the nasal combinations or combinations of /g/ and nasal, and for /k/ in the combinations /pt/, /bs/, /ps/: [asékto] [aksolúto] [konseksjóŋ], seems to be characteristic of the whole area—and others.

Important Sources of Information on the Phonology of Nicaraguan Spanish
(full references in main bibliography)

Books and Articles

Lacayo, Heberto. 1954. Apuntes sobre la pronunciación del español en Nicaragua.
———. 1962. *Cómo pronuncian el español en Nicaragua.*

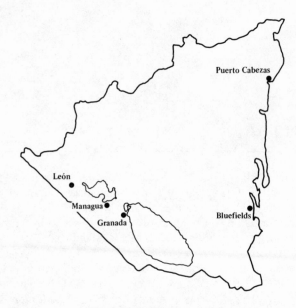

NICARAGUA

Puerto Cabezas

León

Managua

Granada

Bluefields

General tendencies:

/b, d, g/ → [b, d, g] (after another consonant or a
   semivowel)
/s/ → [s] or [θ] ; /s/ syllable final → [h]
Intervocalic /y/ tends to vocalize (*bella* [béi̯a] and
   by hypercorrection, *día* [díi̯a]
/r̄/ → [r̄]
/n/ word final before pause or vowel → [ŋ]
/f/ → [ɸ]
-ado → [áo] ([el merkáo d̸el estáo])

Hypercorrection of *combinaciones cultas:*

nn, nm, mm, gn, gm → [ŋn] or [ŋm] ([iŋnumeráɸle],
   [iŋmed̸iáto], [kolúŋna], [iŋnoránte], [eníŋma])
pt, bs, ps → [kt], [ks], [ks] ([asékto], [aksolúto],
   [konseksjóŋ])

Panama

The Spanish of Panama is another example of what might be termed trade-route language, in that it has the phonological character of those parts of America that were in constant communication with the southern ports of Spain during the colonial period and yet were removed from the viceregal centers of Mexico and Peru. In pronunciation it very much resembles the Spanish of Cuba, Puerto Rico, Venezuela (except the Andes), and the coasts of Colombia.

A closer look at Panamanian Spanish today shows that it has developed what I have chosen to call "attitudinal" features and dichotomies. Group attitudes on the basis of age, education, and urban versus rural residence have become apparent. Alvarado de Ricord (1971) makes distinctions on the basis of the rural/urban dichotomy, on the basis of age, and by education, and Robe (1960), in describing the rural Spanish, had referred to urban differences. It seems to me that there may be a rather strong element of hypercorrection in the urban Spanish of Panama.

Generally Panamanians aspirate /s/ syllable final, and among all speakers the /x/ is [h].

Among the youth of Panama, especially in the cities, /č/ is rendered as [š], and among many urban speakers final /d/ is [t]: [berdát]. While /f/ is almost universally [ɸ] in the countryside, it is often [f] in the cities. Alvarado de Ricord (1971) reports -ado as [aɗo] for Panama City, but most rural and small-town speakers say [ao] or [aw]. Syllable-final /l/ and /r/ are acoustically equivalent or are assimilated to a following consonant in the countryside, but urban speakers of some education apparently attempt to make a distinction. Both [n] and [ŋ] are reported for word-final /n/ before a pause or a vowel, but there is ample evidence of the velar even within the word: [iŋerénte], [koŋsého]. Terrell (1975) reports a very high percentage of deletion of final /n/, with nasalization of the preceding vowel.

Important Sources of Information on the
Phonology of Panamanian Spanish
(full references in main bibliography)

Books and Articles

Robe, Stanley. 1948. "l" and "r" implosives en el español de Panamá.
———. 1960. *The Spanish of rural Panama: Major dialectal features.*
Cohen, Pedro I. 1964. Apuntes sobre la pronunciación del fonema /s/
en Panamá.
———. 1971. *Estudios de lingüística descriptiva: Temas panameños.*
Alvarado de Ricord, Elsie. 1971. *El español de Panamá.*
Revilla, Angel. 1976. Los panameñismos: ¿Una nueva lengua en formación?
Cedergren, Henrietta J. 1978. En torno a la variación de la s final de
sílabe en Panamá: Análisis cuantitativo.

PANAMA

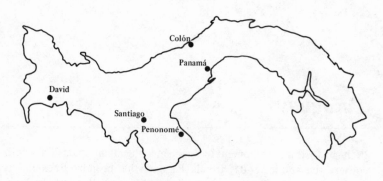

General tendencies:

/x/ → [h] ([hénte], [óho]
/s/ syllable final → [h]

Conflicting testimony of dialectologists seems to indicate "attitudinal" tendencies based on certain parameters: the urban/rural dichotomy, age, education.

/č/ → [š] (youth below twenty-five years of age):
  [mušášo] [nóše]
/d/ word final → [t] (urban); [berɖát]
/f/ → [ɸ] (rural): [ɸóɸoro] [ɸilosoɸía]
-ado → [áo] (rural): [merkáo]
-/l/ and -/r/ acoustically equivalent (rural): [pwélta]
  [pwéṛta]
/n/ word final before pause or vowel → [ŋ] or simply nasalization of preceding vowel: *andén*
  [andéŋ] or [andě̃]

Paraguay

In the historical development of Spanish, Paraguayan Spanish has both conservative and latter-day trends. Paraguay has been landlocked, but many influences have come up the Paraná from the Río de la Plata region. As an example of a conservative trait, one might cite the strict phonemic distinction that has been maintained between /ʎ/ and /y/ while at the same time Paraguay shares with the *porteño* region the aspiration of /s/ syllable final, a development that apparently followed the first settlements in America.

In a nation in which nearly everybody speaks both Spanish and Guaraní, though not necessarily with equal facility, one would expect to find mutual phonological influence. Studies indicate, however, that often too much is assumed in this respect, and certain peculiarities ultimately turn out to be part of the continuum of the Spanish language. Cassano (1972b, 1973b,c) has shown quite convincingly that some of the influences attributed to Guaraní by Malmberg (1947), for instance, are simply part of the evolution of Spanish.

Nevertheless, it is quite possible that a couple of the manners of articulation of Spanish in Paraguay are due to Guaraní influence: the intervocalic /y/ tends to be [ŷ], more alveolar than palatal, a sound that is part of the Guaraní system; and there may be Guaraní influence in the alveolar articulation of /t/ and /d/. Cassano (1972b) has dealt with this at length.

In the case of [ŷ] for /y/, one should recall that this articulation is also common in Antioquia, Colombia, where no Guaraní is spoken.

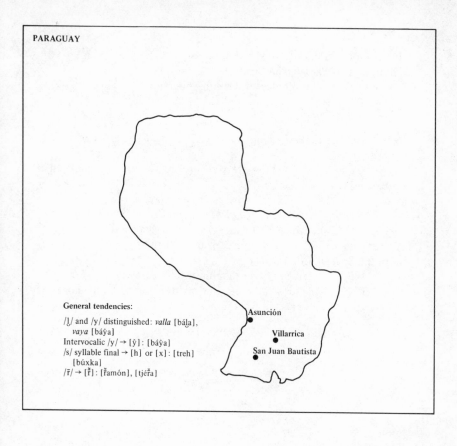

PARAGUAY

General tendencies:

/ĺ/ and /y/ distinguished: *valla* [báḽa],
   vaya [báŷa]
Intervocalic /y/ → [ŷ] : [báŷa]
/s/ syllable final → [h] or [x] : [treh]
   [búxka]
/r̄/ → [ř] : [řamón], [tjéřa]

Asunción

Villarrica

San Juan Bautista

Important Sources of Information on the
Phonology of Paraguayan Spanish
(full references in main bibliography)

Books and Articles

Malmberg, Bertil. 1947. *Notas sobre la fonética del español en el Paraguay.*
Gáspari, Luis de. 1964. Presente y futuro de la lengua española en el Paraguay.
Rubin, Joan. 1968*a*. Bilingual usage in Paraguay.
———. 1968*b*. *National bilingualism in Paraguay.*
———. 1968*c*. Language and education in Paraguay.
Cassano, Paul. 1972*b*. The alveolarization of the /n/, /t/, /d/ and /rt/ in the Spanish of Paraguay.
———. 1973*b*. Retention of certain hiatuses in Paraguayan Spanish.
———. 1973*c*. The substrat theory in relation to the bilingualism of Paraguay: Problems and findings.

Peru

The Spanish phonology of Peru is quite conservative in terms of the historical evolution of the language. Lima, the northern coast, and certain other coastal points are exceptions in some respects. Escobar (1976), while writing of bilingualism and dialectology in Peru, insists that the circumstance of the presence of millions of Quechua-speakers in the population makes for the formation of two dialects beyond the usual considerations: that of the initial bilingual and that of the advanced bilingual.

Since the Quechua of the area has three vowels, [I, a, U], there is a tendency among speakers of the highlands to heighten the Spanish /e/ and /o/, or to hypercorrect: *¿Qué es eso?* may sound like [kI:sIsU]. It would be a mistake, however, to attribute to the Quechua substratum all the consonantal dialect features of Peruvian Spanish, which may exist in several places where Quechua is not spoken.

The distinction between the phonemes /ļ/ and /y/ as [ļ] and [y] is maintained in most of the highlands. The tense grooved /s/ [s] is the rule except in some coastal areas. In the highlands -*ado* is still [aḍo], and the /r̄/ is often assibilated as [r̃]. Vowel reduction is also fairly common in the Sierra: *Potosí* [potsí], *partes* [párts].

Recordings I made in 1958 of Lima schoolchildren and of a few adults show trends toward a more "relaxed" coastal type of articulation in the younger generation. They were all *yeísta,* they often aspirated the /s/ syllable final: [eḥ mwi ǵránde], [loḥ grándeh]. -*ado* was very often [ao], and the intervocalic /b/, /d/, /g/ were hardly audible in many cases. They did, however, have the vowel reduction referred to.

**Important Sources of Information on the
Phonology of Peruvian Spanish**
(full references in main bibliography)

Books and Articles

Benvenutto Murrieta, Pedro. 1936. *El lenguaje peruano,* vol. 1.
Canfield, D. Lincoln. 1960*b*. Lima Castilian: The pronunciation of
Spanish in the City of the Kings.
Navarro Maraví, Aurelio R. 1964. La pronunciación en los pueblos del
centro del Perú.
Escobar, Alberto. 1976. Bilingualism and dialectology in Peru.
———. 1977. ¿Existe el castellano limeño?

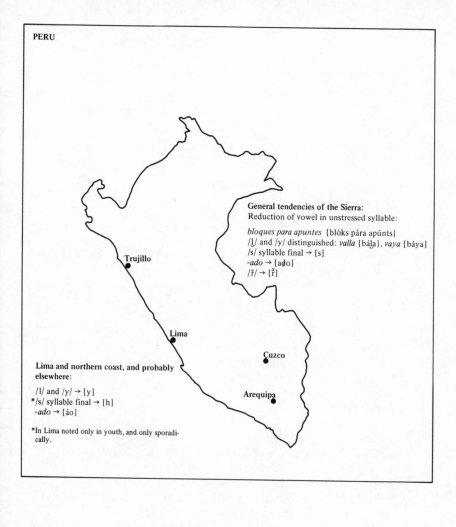

PERU

Trujillo

Lima

Cuzco

Arequipa

General tendencies of the Sierra:
Reduction of vowel in unstressed syllable:

bloques para apuntes [blóks pára apúnts]
/ḷ/ and /y/ distinguished: *valla* [báḷa], *vaya* [báya]
/s/ syllable final → [s]
-ado → [aḋo]
/r̄/ → [ř]

Lima and northern coast, and probably
elsewhere:

/l/ and /y/ → [y]
*/s/ syllable final → [h]
-ado → [áo]

*In Lima noted only in youth, and only sporadi-
cally.

Puerto Rico

The island of Puerto Rico has been more thoroughly studied linguistically than any other political entity of America, except perhaps Colombia, principally owing to the efforts of Tomás Navarro Tomás, whose *El español en Puerto Rico* was published by the University of Puerto Rico in 1948. The fieldwork had been done in the academic year 1926–27. Perhaps inspired by this, there have been many subsequent studies of Puerto Rican Spanish. Rubén del Rosario (1946, 1955) and Resnick (1975, bibliography) give evidence of this.

Navarro's work on Puerto Rico, which is still the most reliable, actually "discovers" features that are to be found in several other places later and prepares subsequent investigators for the polymorphism that was to be documented there and elsewhere in more recent times. However, as Del Rosario (1958) points out, there has been much social mobility since Navarro's 1926–27 fieldwork, and Navarro used only one informant from each locale.

The phonology of Puerto Rican Spanish is "latter-day" in terms of the evolution of the Andalusian dialect of Castilian, but it exhibits certain developments that are not recorded in Spain itself.

Characteristic of most speakers of the island are the /x/ as [h], and the /s/ syllable final as [h] or [∅], and the word-final /n/ before a vowel or a pause as [ŋ].

Except for sections of San Sebastián, Lares, and Las Marías in western Puerto Rico, there is a strong tendency toward acoustic equivalence of /l/ and /r/ syllable final, and though it is often difficult to identify the sound as either [l] or [r], the general impression given is that of [l]. Navarro Tomás (1948) found, however, that in the Southwest the impression is that of [r], and in the Northeast that of a mixed sound [ɭ]. The word *puerta* may be heard as [pwélta], less often as [pwérta], and sometimes actually as neither, but as [pwéɭta].

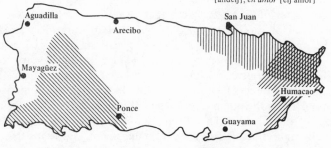

General tendencies:

/č/ → [tj] : [la létje]

/x/ → [h] : [hénte], [óho]

/s/ syllable final → [h] or [Ø] : *dos pescados* [doh pehkáoh],* [do pekáo]

/n/ word final before pause or vowel → [ŋ] : *andén* [andéŋ], *en amor* [eŋ amór]

▨ /r̄/ → [r̄]

▨ -/l/ and -/ɾ/ → [l] or [r] or [ɫ] : [pwélta], [pwérta], [pwéɫta]

▥ /r̄/ → [xr] : *carro* [káxro]

▨ /r̄/ → [R̥] (or [R]) : [káR̥o]

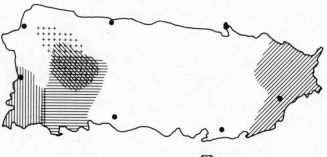

▨ /s/ → [ṡ]

▤ /č/ → [č]

▥ Focal area of -/l/ and -/ɾ/ → [r]

☐ Area of -/l/ and -/ɾ/ → [l]

⊞ -/l/ and -/ɾ/ as distinct phonemes: *alto* [álto], *harto* [árto]

▨ -/l/ and /ɾ/ → [l] or [r] or [ɫ] : [pwélta], [pwérta], [pwéɫta]

*Actually there is compensatory lengthening of the consonant: [pekkáo]

Since /l/ and /r/ are somewhat neutralized, along with /s/ syllable final, /b/, /d/, and /g/ tend to be occlusive more often than would otherwise be the case after these consonants: *verdad* [beldá], *desde* [déhde], or [dehɖe], *Margarita* [maⱡgaríta].

In all of Puerto Rico except parts of the Southwest (Lajas, Sabana Grande, Maricao, Lares), the /č/ tends to be [tj]: [nótje], [mutjátjo]. [létje]. In the Southwest it is [č], and one notes today, as in Cuba, a tendency toward [š] at times.

In the matter of /r̄/, at the time that Navarro did his fieldwork, practically all of the country had the velar articulation [R̥], which could be transcribed as [x]. The Southwest had the traditional alveolar trill [r̄], and the northeast coast, including San Juan, tended toward the mixed variety, which begins with a velar fricative, voiceless, and ends with a single or multiple vibrant. Interesting theories have been proposed on the origin of the velar. Zlotchew (1974) believes it grew out of the mixed variety: from [r̄] to a voiceless [r̥̄] to [xr] to [x], usually transcribed [R̥] to keep it "in the family." He seems to believe it is of rather recent origin, based on experiences in labor camps with migrant workers in upstate New York during the past twenty years. Megenney (1978) disposes of the theory of black origins by showing that it is most common in Puerto Rico where there are few blacks but are great numbers of *jíbaros,* who were the products of the native Indians and the Spaniards. Navarro Tomás (1948) also conjectures that it may have been a native accommodation to the Castilian sound. It may be that, with recent social mobility, the *jíbaro* has moved in greater numbers to New York and other places where he was not much in evidence before.

In Lares and some of the surrounding country /s/ was [š] at the time Navarro did his investigations. The usual /s/ of Puerto Rico is dorsoalveolar as far as the blade of the tongue is concerned, and apicodental with regard to the point. There is generally little grooving, and at times it becomes so *plana* that there is a lisping effect. /s/ syllable final tends to be aspirated or dropped entirely. This is true to such an extent that speakers will hypercorrect, adding -/s/ where there is none. The impression of speed in the speech of Puerto Ricans and others of the Caribbean may be enhanced by the deletion of -/s/. A Mexican pronouncing *estos son los dos pescados fritos* may take longer than one who says: [éhtoh son loh doh pehkáo frítoh].

Important Sources of Information on the
Phonology of Puerto Rican Spanish
(full references in main bibliography)

Bibliographies

El español en Puerto Rico: Bibliografía. 1971. [Universidad de Puerto Rico].

Books and Articles

Del Rosario, Rubén. 1946. La lengua de Puerto Rico.

Navarro Tomás, Tomás. 1948. *El español en Puerto Rico.*

Del Rosario, Rubén. 1958. *Consideraciones sobre la lengua en Puerto Rico.*

Matluck, Joseph. 1961. Fonemas finales en el consonantismo puertorriqueño.

Granda, Germán de. 1966. La velarización de "rr" en el español de Puerto Rico.

Figueroa Berríos, Edwin. 1971. Habla y folklore en Ponce.

Zlotchew, Clark M. 1974. The transformation of the multiple vibrant to the fricative velar in the Spanish of Puerto Rico.

Corrientes actuales en la dialectología del Caribe hispánico. 1978.

Guitart, Jorge M. 1978. A propósito del español de Cuba y Puerto Rico: Hacia un modelo sociolingüístico de lo sociodialectal.

Hammond, Robert M. 1978. An experimental verification of the phonemic status of open and closed vowels in Caribbean Spanish.

Megenney, William W. 1978. El problema de "R" velar en Puerto Rico.

Terrell, Tracy D. 1978*b*. Sobre la aspiración y elisión de /S/ implosiva y final en el español de Puerto Rico.

Vaquero de Ramírez, María. 1978. Hacia una espectrografía dialectal: El fonema /č/ en Puerto Rico.

The United States

Among the foreign languages taught in the schools of the United States, Spanish holds first place at all levels. Not only is the language taught extensively, it is spoken as a first language by some fifteen million people who are American citizens.

The main nuclei of Spanish speech in the United States are northern New Mexico/southern Colorado, the border territories from California through Texas, the Florida peninsula, New York City, and other large cities of the Northeast and Midwest. Only one of these, the New Mexico/Colorado dialect area, has maintained linguistic continuity since colonial days, and its speech goes back to about 1600. The other centers of Spanish represent immigrations of more recent times from northern and central Mexico, from Cuba, and from Puerto Rico, with a few from Spain and other Spanish American regions. It would be fair to say that most of these speakers of Spanish in the United States are now bilingual, and in many areas Spanish is losing ground to English, especially in vocabulary. It has been my experience, having lived in all these areas of Spanish speech, that, of the people who have Spanish names, many actually speak English in preference to Spanish, some speak no Spanish, and some think in English when they speak Spanish. It is not a question, therefore, of a phalanx of Spanish-speaking people.

The Spanish of the northern New Mexico/southern Colorado dialect area resembles that of Guatemala and Costa Rica more than that of neighboring Mexico because it represents a similar stage in the evolution of Andalusian Castilian. There is a tendency to vocalize intervocalic /y/ or leave it out entirely: *capilla* [kapía], *ella* [éia] or [éa]; /r̄/ is often assibilated as it is in Guatemala and Costa Rica: *rica tierra* [r̃íka tjér̃a]; /x/ is [h]: *paja* [páha], *gente* [hénte], and, like *salvadoreños*, the New Mexican often aspirates /s/ syllable final. Historically this Spanish is of a later time than that of the Mexican plateau, which came bodily into the border area in the nineteenth and twentieth centuries.

The border strip from California through southern Texas has a Spanish that in phonology represents that of sixteenth-century Andalusia and the regions of Extremadura settled from there. It was nurtured in central Mexico and brought to Texas, Arizona, southern New Mexico, and California since independence, for the most part. This border Spanish does not aspirate /s/ syllable final to the extent that the New Mexico/Colorado region does. The /r̄/ tends to be [r̄], and /x/ is generally [x̌], with a tendency toward [h] in some areas, probably owing to English influence.

Had there been a continuity of isolated Florida Spanish from the days of Juan Ponce de León and Hernando de Soto, the Castilian of Saint Augustine might sound very much like that of Mexico. But there was no such continuity, and the Spanish of Florida today is a result of transplants of the nineteenth and twentieth centuries, with three main centers—Key West, Tampa, and Miami—although there are quite a few groups in other parts of the state, such as Jacksonville, Daytona Beach, and the university cities of Tallahassee and Gainesville.

Key West Spanish, according to Beardsley (1972-73), has been in Florida since the middle of the nineteenth century, moving in from Cuba, and apparently shows more conservative phonological features than that brought to Miami a hundred years later.

Long after the establishment of Fort Brooke in 1823 and the Civil War blockade, the building of the South Florida Railroad brought growth to Tampa, and labor troubles in Key West brought a cigar industry with thousands of Spanish and Cuban employees. The colony founded in Tampa by Vicente Martínez Ybor had some thirty thousand inhabitants by the middle of the twentieth century, and, though there were signs of absorption by the Anglo community, a spillover from the Miami area of refugees from Castro's Cuba may tend to perpetuate the Hispanic colony.

The study of Canfield (1951a) indicates roughly three manifestations of Tampa Spanish: (1) that of northern Spain (Asturias or Galicia), with distinction between /ʎ/ and /y/ and between /θ/ and /ś/ (apicoalveolar), a uvular /x/ and a deeper tone in the general flow of speech; (2) a transitional type, influenced by English and Cuban Spanish, in which the /θ/ was more like that of English (less volume of air than the Spanish), the /s/ was no longer apicoalveolar, and the /x/ had moved from uvular to laryngeal; (3) a Spanish very much like that of the streets of Havana, Cuba, with aspirated /s/ syllable final, an /x/

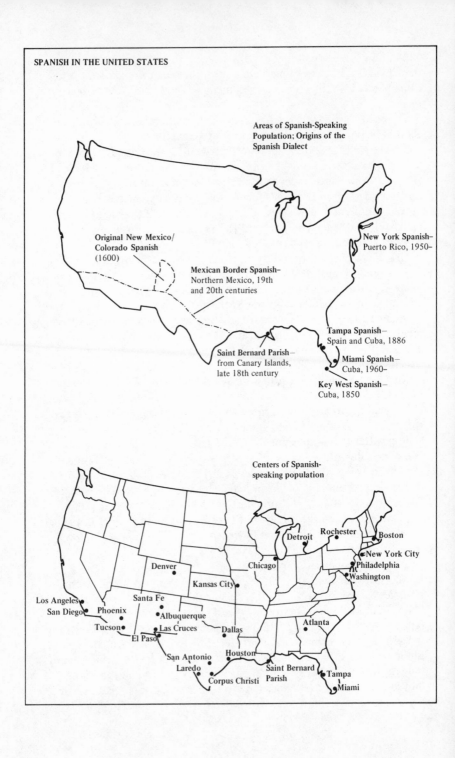

SPANISH IN THE UNITED STATES

Areas of Spanish-Speaking
Population; Origins of the
Spanish Dialect

Original New Mexico/
Colorado Spanish
(1600)

New York Spanish–
Puerto Rico, 1950–

Mexican Border Spanish–
Northern Mexico, 19th
and 20th centuries

Tampa Spanish–
Spain and Cuba, 1886

Saint Bernard Parish–
from Canary Islands,
late 18th century

Miami Spanish–
Cuba, 1960–

Key West Spanish–
Cuba, 1850

Centers of Spanish-
speaking population

Detroit

Rochester

Boston

New York City

Chicago

Philadelphia

Washington

Denver

Kansas City

Los Angeles

Santa Fe

San Diego

Phoenix

Albuquerque

Atlanta

Tucson

Las Cruces

Dallas

El Paso

San Antonio

Houston

Laredo

Saint Bernard
Parish

Tampa

Corpus Christi

Miami

SOME PHONOLOGICAL FEATURES OF UNITED STATES SPANISH

⊟ /r̄/ tends to be [řǰ] (also heard in Guatemala, Costa Rica, the Eastern Cordillera of Colombia, the highlands of Ecuador, Peru, and Bolivia, Paraguay, northwestern Argentina, Chile)

▓ /r̄/ tends to be [R̥] (also heard in Puerto Rico, the Dominican Republic, northern Colombian coast, some in Panama)

▥ /y/ intervocalic tends to be [i̯] (also heard in all of Central America except Panama, the coasts of Colombia, and Ecuador)

▨ -/s/ tends to be [h], sporadically [Ø] (also heard in all of the Caribbean islands, in Venezuela except Táchira, Mérida, Trujillo, the coasts of Colombia and Ecuador, the northern coast of Peru, Paraguay, most of Argentina (except Santiago del Estero and the northwest), the llanos of Bolivia, and all of Chile)

▧ /l/ and /r/ syllable final tend to be acoustically equivalent (also heard in Puerto Rico, the Dominican Republic, Venezuela—except the Andes—the coasts of Colombia, Ecuador, rural Panama, central Chile, some in western Cuba) that is also a mere aspiration [h], and a velar /n/ word final before a pause or a vowel: *van a cantar* [baŋ a kantár], *pan* [paŋ].

The Spanish of Miami and its Saugüesera (southwest area) is essentially that of Cuba in 1960, mainly Havana. Historically it is Andalusian Castilian of the late colonial period and presents an interesting contrast to the Spanish of highland Bolivia, for example. Phonologically, it is of lax consonantal articulation, with the aspiration of /s/ syllable final very common and a *jota* (/x/) that is always of laryngeal quality and that corresponds phonetically to the aspirated /s/. The /n/ word final before a vowel or pause is [ŋ] in most cases, though Terrell (1975*b*) indicates that it may be [n] in these situations, or it may be deleted in favor of a nasalized vowel: *son* [sõ]. Haden and Matluck (1973) point out that there is some tendency to level syllable-final /l/ and /r/ in favor of the former, but the trend is not nearly so strong as in Puerto Rico. It has been my experience that many Cubans, especially women, tend to unvoice /r̄/ [r̥].

New York City represents another large contingent of Spanish-speakers, and this language is the second one to English that is heard as one walks the streets of the great metropolis. The Spanish-speakers of New York come from several countries of Latin America and from Spain itself, but the dominant group linguistically is Puerto Rican. It should be noted, too, that thousands of Puerto Ricans are found in cities of the East and Midwest. Many have moved from New York City to sections of New Jersey and Pennsylvania, to the fruit area of upstate New York (Rochester had thirty thousand at one time), to Detroit and Chicago, and to many other cities. It is to be noted, also, that in areas where the Spanish-speaking population is not dense, the children of the original settlers tend to abandon Spanish in favor of English.

Raymond MacCurdy (1950) takes us to another manifestation of United States Spanish, Saint Bernard Parish, Louisiana, where Spanish-speakers settled very late in the eighteenth century from the Caribbean and, originally, the Canary Islands. The dialect exhibits traits of late Andalusian Spanish, and the people are often referred to as *isleños*.

Sephardic Spanish (Dzhudezmo, Ladino, Judeo-Spanish) is to be heard in New York City and in other places in the United States, and although there were a great many Sephardim at one time, Teschner, Bills, and Craddock (1975, p. xx) believe that today there are not more than fifteen thousand. Many of us have known Sephardic Jews, some of them merchants and professionals, and we have observed how the language has been lost in the second or third generation, as has also happened with Yiddish, a dialect of High German.

The story of the expulsion of the Spanish Jews after the edict of Ferdinand and Isabella, signed in 1492, is well known, as is the fact that the cities of the old Turkish empire became havens for many of these Spanish-speaking Jews. After waves of nationalism in Turkey and in the Balkans, many migrated to the New World. As might be expected, in Spanish America they assimilate linguistically to modern Spanish.

The consonantal phoneme structure of Judeo-Spanish is much richer than that of modern Spanish, since it reflects the status of the late fifteenth century, before the extensive leveling of the period following:

$$/p/ \quad /b/ \quad /v/ \quad /t/ \quad /d/ \quad /k/ \quad /g/$$
$$/f/ \quad /s/ \quad /z/ \quad /š/ \quad /ž/ \quad /y/ \quad (/h/)$$
$$/č/$$
$$/m/ \quad /n/ \quad /ñ/$$
$$/l/$$
$$/r/ \quad /ř/$$

Apparently ǰ occurs as an allophone of /ž/ initially and after /n/.

Important Sources of Information on the
Phonology of United States Spanish
(full references in main bibliography)

Bibliographies

Solé, Carlos. 1970. *Bibliografía sobre el español en América: 1920–1967.*
Teschner, Richard V.; Bills, Garland D.; and Craddock, Jerry R. 1975. *Spanish and English of United States Hispanos: A critical, annotated, linguistic bibliography.*
Woodbridge, Hensley C. 1977. Fourteen Chicano bibliographies, 1971–1975.

General

Canfield, D. Lincoln. 1976. *Rasgos fonológicos del castellano en los Estados Unidos.*

Northern New Mexico/Southern Colorado

Espinosa, Aurelio M. 1909. Studies in New Mexican Spanish.

Rael, Juan B. 1937. A study of the phonology and morphology of New Mexico Spanish based on a collection of 410 folk-tales.

Bowen, J. Donald. 1952. The Spanish of San Antonito, New Mexico.

Mexican Border

Post, Anita C. 1934. Southern Arizona Spanish phonology.

Tsuzaki, Stanley M. 1963. English influence in the phonology and morphology of the Spanish spoken in the Mexican colony in Detroit.

Coltharp, Lurline H. 1965. *The tongue of the Tirilones.*

Phillips, Robert N., Jr. 1967. Los Angeles Spanish.

González, Gustavo. 1969. *The phonology of Corpus Christi Spanish.*

Cárdenas, Daniel. 1970. *Dominant Spanish dialect spoken in the United States.*

Ornstein, Jacob. 1971. Language varieties along the United States–Mexican border.

———. 1972. Toward a classification of southwest Spanish nonstandard variants.

Marroco, Mary Ann Wilkinson. 1972. The Spanish of Corpus Christi.

González, Gustavo. 1973. The analysis of Chicano Spanish and the problem of usage.

Poulter, Virgil L. 1973. A phonological study of the speech of Mexican-American college students native to Ft. Worth–Dallas.

Rodríguez del Pino, Salvador. 1973. El idioma de Aztlán: Una lengua que surge.

Matluck, Joseph, and Mace, Betty J. 1973. Language characteristics of Mexican-American children.

Phillips, Robert N., Jr. 1975. Southwestern Spanish: A descriptive analysis.

Hannum, Thomasina. 1978. Attitudes of bilingual students toward Spanish.

Valdés Fallis, Guadalupe. 1978. A comprehensive approach to the teaching of Spanish to bilingual Spanish-speaking students.

Florida Spanish

Canfield, D. Lincoln. 1951a. Tampa Spanish: Three characters in search of a pronunciation.

Beardsley, Theodore S., Jr. 1972–73. Influencias angloamericanas en el español de Cayo Hueso.

Haden, Ernest F., and Matluck, Joseph. 1973. El habla culta de la Habana: Análisis fonológico preliminar. (Made through Cuban informants in Miami.)

New York City and Other Eastern Cities

Decker, Bob Dan. 1952. Phonology of the Puerto Rican Spanish of Lorain, Ohio: A study in the environmental displacement of a dialect.

Casiano Montáñez, Lucrecia. 1965. La pronunciación de los puertorriqueños en Nueva York.

Fishman, Joshua A., and Herasimchuk, Eleanor. 1969. The multiple prediction of phonological variables in a bilingual speech community.

Sephardic Spanish

Luria, Max A. 1930. Judeo-Spanish dialects in New York City.

Umphrey, G. W., and Adatto, Emma. 1936. Linguistic archaism of the Seattle Sephardim.

Agard, Frederick B. 1950. Present day Judaeo-Spanish in the United States.

Hirsch, Ruth. 1951. A study of some aspects of a Judeo-Spanish dialect as spoken by a New York Sephardic family.

Estrugo, José M. 1958. *Los sefardíes.*

Crews, Cynthia. 1962. Reflections on Judaeo-Spanish by a Spanish Jew.

Besso, Henry V. 1964. Situación actual del judeo-español.

Sala, Marius. 1972. Los fonemas /š/, /ž/ en el judeoespañol.

Saint Bernard Parish, Louisiana

MacCurdy, Raymond R. 1950. *The Spanish dialect of St. Bernard Parish, Louisiana.*

Uruguay

Except for the *fronterizo* situation, where Portuguese intrudes in varying degrees on the Spanish of Uruguay (as depicted on the accompanying map), the phonology of Uruguayan Spanish is virtually identical to that of the *porteño* region of Argentina.

As in Buenos Aires, the /x/ of Uruguay tends to be [x] rather than [h], and even the aspirated /s/ syllable final may take on palatal friction in line with the articulation of /x/, Such a word as *busca* is often pronounced [búxka], while the allophone of *los dos* will be more akin to an aspiration.

The /ř/ of the area is [ř] and does not have the assibilated character of nearby Misiones and Corrientes, Argentina, or of Paraguay: *Ramón* [řamón]; *garra* [gářa].

As in a good part of eastern Argentina and in sections of the Northwest, both /ļ/ and /y/ of the traditional sound system have become [ž], with a tendency toward unvoicing in recent times, especially among women.

The Uruguayan linguist Ricci (1967) has given us a careful examination of the often repeated concept of the Italian contamination of River Plate Spanish, and he ultimately discounts all but lexical influence except in the early stages of the languages-in-contact situation. His broad understanding of developments in other Hispanic regions makes this possible.

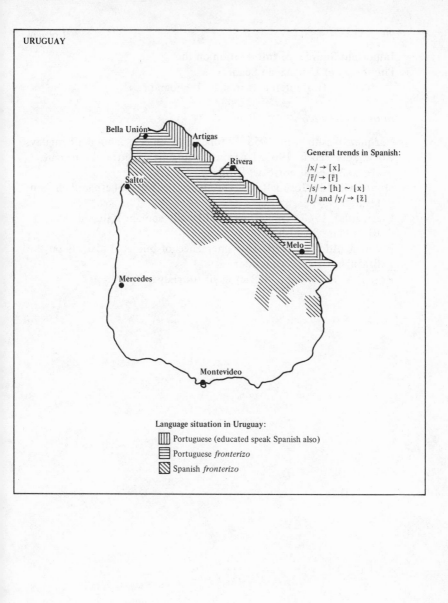

URUGUAY

Bella Unión

Artigas

Rivera

Salto

General trends in Spanish:

$/x/ \to [x]$
$/\bar{r}/ \to [\bar{r}]$
$-/s/ \to [h] \sim [x]$
$/\mathfrak{l}/$ and $/y/ \to [\check{z}]$

Melo

Mercedes

Montevideo

Language situation in Uruguay:

▥ Portuguese (educated speak Spanish also)

▤ Portuguese *fronterizo*

▨ Spanish *fronterizo*

Important Sources of Information on the
Phonology of Uruguayan Spanish
(full references in main bibliography)

Books and Articles

Vázquez, Wáshington. 1953. El fonema /s/ en el español del Uruguay.
Rona, José Pedro. 1963. La frontera lingüística entre el portugués y
el español en el norte del Uruguay.
Montes Giraldo, José J. 1966. Observaciones sobre el español en Montevideo.
Ricci, Julio. 1967. The influence of locally spoken Italian dialects on
River Plate Spanish.
Elizaicín, Adolfo. 1976. The emergence of bilingual dialects on the
Brazilian-Uruguayan border.
Rosell, A. 1978. Sobre dialectología uruguaya.

Venezuela

The phonological pattern of Venezuela, except for the Andean states of Mérida, Táchira, and Trujillo, is for the most part that of the Caribbean, and therefore, late Andalusian.

One general feature is the articulation of /x/ as [h], as in all of Colombia.

In all but the Andean section, the /s/ syllable final is often aspirated or dropped: *buscan unas hojas verdes* [búhkaŋ únah óhah ꞵéɬdeh].

The -/l/ and -/r/ tend to be acoustically equivalent in most of the country and are heard as [l], as [r], and as]ɬ] or, in the case of a following consonant, are not heard but the following consonant is doubled: *carne* [kárne], [kálne], [káɬne], [kánne]. The /r̄/ is generally [r̄], and /n/ word final before a pause or a vowel is generally [ŋ].

In the three states of Táchira, Mérida, and Trujillo the articulation is more like that of highland Colombia across the border. Syllable-final /s/, /l/, and /r/ are distinguished and clearly pronounced.

Important Sources of Information on the
Phonology of Venezuelan Spanish
(full references in main bibliography)

Books and Articles

Hauser, Guido. 1947. La pronunciación del castellano en Venezuela: Un reflejo de la continuidad romance.

Alonso, Amado. 1953. *Estudios lingüísticos: Temas hispanoamericanos.*

Ocampo Marín, Jaime. 1968. *Notas sobre el español hablado en Mérida.*

Terrell, Tracy D. 1977*b*. Aspiration and deletion of word final /s/ in the Spanish of Caracas, Venezuela.

Corrientes actuales en la dialectología del Caribe hispánico. 1978.

Hammond, Robert M. 1978. An experimental verification of the phonemic status of open and closed vowels in Caribbean Spanish.

VENEZUELA

Andean states of Táchira, Mérida, Trujillo:

⊟ /n/ word final after pause or vowel → [n] ;
-/s/ → [s] : -/l/ and -/r/ distinct

Tendencies in the rest of Venezuela:

/s/ → [s] or [θ]
/s/ syllable final → [h] or [Ø] : [doh pehkáoh] , [do pekkáo]
-/l/ and -/r/ leveled to [l] or [ɬ] : [pwélta], [pwéɬta]
/n/ word final before pause or vowel → [ŋ] : [andéŋ]

General Bibliography

Agard, Frederick B. 1950. Present day Judaeo-Spanish in the United States. *Hispania* 33:203-10.

Agüero, Arturo. 1964. El español en Costa Rica y su atlas lingüístico. In *Presente y futuro de la lengua española*, 1:135-52. Madrid: OFINES.

Alarcos Llorach, Emilio. 1964. Algunas cuestiones fonológicas del español de hoy. In *Presente y futuro de la lengua española*, 2:151-61. Madrid: OFINES.

Albor, Hugo. 1971. Observaciones sobre la fonología del español hablado en Nariño. *Thesaurus* 26:1-19.

Alonso, Amado. 1925. El grupo "tr" en España y América. *Homenaje a Menéndez Pidal* 2:167-91.

———. 1939. Examen de la teoría indigenista de Rodolfo Lenz. *BA/RFH* 1:313-50.

———. 1945. Geografía fonética: "-l" y "-r" implosivas en español. *BA/RFH* 7:313-45.

———. 1951. La *ll* y sus alteraciones en España y América. *Estudios dedicados a Menéndez Pidal* 2:41-89.

———. 1953. *Estudios lingüísticos: Temas hispanoamericanos.* Madrid: Gredos.

Alvar, Manuel. 1966-67. Polimorfismo y otros aspectos fonéticos en el habla de Santo Tomás Ajusco. *Anuario de Letras* 6:11-42.

———. 1969. Nuevas notas sobre el español de Yucatán. *Ibero-romania* 1:159-89.

Alvarado de Ricord, Elsie. 1971. *El español de Panamá.* Panama: Universidad de Panamá.

Alvarez Nazario. 1961. *El elemento afronegroide en el español de Puerto Rico.* San Juan.

Atlas lingüístico de la Península Ibérica (ALPI). 1962. Vol. 1. *Fonética.* Madrid: CSIC.

Atlas lingüístico etnográfico de Colombia (ALEC). 1970-75. *Noticias*

Culturales (Bogotá: Instituto Caro y Cuervo), nos. 108–49; 159–78.

Avila, Raúl. 1966–67. Fonemas vocálicos en el español de Tamazunchale. *Anuario de Letras* 6:61–80.

Ayala Gauna, B. Velmiro. 1963. El español de Corrientes. *Boletín de Filología* 10:115–26.

Bartoš, Lubomir. 1967. La realización de los grafemas B y V en el español actual con respecto a la modalidad cubana. *Ibero-americana Pragensia* 1:55–66.

Beardsley, Theodore S., Jr. 1972–73. Influencias angloamericanas en el español de Cayo Hueso. *Exilio* 6:4/7:87–100.

———. 1975. French R in Caribbean Spanish? *Revista/Review Interamericana* 5:101–9.

———. 1976. Bibliografía preliminar de estudios sobre el español en los Estados Unidos. *Boletín de la Academia Norteamericana de la Lengua Española* 1:49–73.

Becerra Coy, Servio. 1973. Introducción a la fonología de las consonantes finales de sílaba en el español de Cartagena de Indias. Ph.D. diss., University of Wisconsin.

Benvenutto Murrieta, Pedro. 1936. *El lenguaje peruano,* vol. 1 (Lima, Peru).

Berk-Seligson, Susan and Seligson, Mitchell A. 1979. The phonological correlates of social stratification in the Spanish of Costa Rica. *Lingua* 46:1–28.

Bertot, Lillian. 1969. A descriptive phonological study of the Spanish spoken in the province of Havana, Cuba. M.A. thesis, Florida Atlantic University.

Besso, Henry V. 1964. Situación actual del judeo-español. In *Presente y futuro de la lengua española,* 2:307–24. Madrid: OFINES.

Bickerton, Derek, and Escalante, Aquilas. 1970. Palenquero: A Spanish-based Creole of northern Colombia. *Lingua* 24:254–67.

Bolinger, Dwight L. 1952. Evidence on X. *Hispania* 35:49–63.

———. 1961. Acento melódico. Acento de intensidad. *Boletín de Filología* (Santiago: Universidad de Chile) 13:33–48.

Bowen, J. Donald. 1952. The Spanish of San Antonito, New Mexico. Ph.D. disser., University of New Mexico.

———. 1955. The phonemic interpretation of semivowels in Spanish. *Language* 31:236–40.

Boyd-Bowman, Peter. 1952*a*. Sobre restos de lleísmo en México. *NRFH* 6:69–74.

———. 1952*b*. La pérdida de vocales átonas en la planicie mexicana. *NRFH* 6:138–40.

———. 1953. Sobre la pronunciación del español en el Ecuador. *NRFH* 7:221–33.

———. 1956. The regional origins of the earliest Spanish colonists of America. *PMLA* 71:1152–72.

———. 1960. *El habla de Guanajuato.* Mexico: Universidad Nacional Autónoma de México.

———. 1964. *Indice geobiográfico de 40,000 pobladores españoles de América en el siglo XVI, 1493–1519.* Vol. 1, Bogotá: Instituto Caro y Cuervo; vol. 2 (1968), Mexico: Editorial Jus.

———. 1968. Regional origins of Spanish colonists of America: 1540–1559. *Buffalo Studies* 4:3–26.

———. 1972. La emigración española a América: 1540–1579. *Studia hispanica in honorem R. Lapesa* (Madrid: Gredos) 2:123–47.

Buesa Oliver, Tomás, and Flórez, Luis. 1956. *Atlas lingüístico de Colombia (ALEC): Cuestionario preliminar.* Bogotá: Instituto Caro y Cuervo.

Canellada de Zamora, María J., and Zamora, Alonso V. 1960. Vocales caducas en el español mexicano. *NRFH* 14:221–24.

Canfield, D. Lincoln. 1934. *Spanish literature in Mexican languages as a source for the study of Spanish pronunciation.* New York: Instituto de las Españas.

———. 1951*a*. Tampa Spanish: Three characters in search of a pronunciation. *Modern Language Journal* 35:42–44.

———. 1951*b*. Guatemalan *rr* and *s:* A recapitulation of Old Spanish sibilant gradation. *Florida State University Studies in Modern Languages and Literatures* 3:49–51.

———. 1952. Spanish American data for the chronology of sibilant changes. *Hispania* 35:25–30.

———. 1953*a*. Andalucismos en la pronunciación salvadoreña. *Hispania* 36:32–33.

———. 1953*b*. La pronunciación del español en el Salvador. *Comunicaciones del Instituto de Investigaciones Científicas* (San Salvador). April, pp. 28–32.

———. 1960*a*. Observaciones sobre el español salvadoreño. *Filología* (Buenos Aires) 6:29–76.

———. 1960*b*. Lima Castilian: The pronunciation of Spanish in the City of the Kings. *Romance Notes* 2:1–4.

———. 1962*a*. *La pronunciación del español en América: Ensayo histórico-descriptivo.* Bogotá: Instituto Caro y Cuervo.

———. 1962*b*. Observaciones sobre la pronunciación del castellano en Colombia. *Hispania* 45:247–48.

———. 1964. The diachronic dimension of synchronic Hispanic dialectology. *Linguistics* 7:5–9.

———. 1967. Trends in American Castilian. *Hispania* 50:912–18.

———. 1968*a*. *East meets West, south of the border: Essays on Spanish American life and attitudes.* Carbondale: Southern Illinois University Press.

———. 1968*b*. La tenacidad estructural del castellano americano. *Revista Hispánica Moderna* 34:564–69.

———. 1975. Spanish in Florida. *Hispanic influences in the United States* (New York: Spanish Institute), pp. 15–20.

———. 1976. Rasgos fonológicos del castellano en los Estados Unidos. *Boletín de la Academia Norteamericana de la lengua española* 1:17–23.

———. 1978. La identificación de dialectos del español americano a base de rasgos distintivos. In *Homenaje a Fernando Antonio Martínez.* Bogotá: Instituto Caro y Cuervo.

Cárdenas, Daniel. 1955. The Spanish of Jalisco. *PMLA* 70:556–61.

———. 1958. Geographical distribution of the assibilated R, RR in Spanish America. *Orbis* 7:407–14.

———. 1967. El español de Jalisco: Contribución a la geografía lingüística hispanoamericana. *Revista de Filología Española.* Anejo 85.

———. 1970. *Dominant Spanish dialect spoken in the United States.* Washington, D.C.: Center for Applied Linguistics.

Casiano Montáñez, Lucrecia. 1965. La pronunciación de los puertorriqueños en Nueva York. M.A. thesis, University of Puerto Rico.

Cassano, Paul V. 1972*a*. The French influence on the Spanish of the River Plate. *Orbis* 21:174–82.

———. 1972*b*. The alveolarization of the /n/, /t/, /d/ and /rt/ in the Spanish of Paraguay. *Linguistics* 93:22–26.

———. 1973*a*. The influence of American English on the phonology of American Spanish. *Orbis* 22:201–14.

———. 1973*b*. Retention of certain hiatuses in Paraguayan Spanish. *Linguistics* 109:12–16.

———. 1973*c*. The substrat theory in relation to the bilingualism of Paraguay: Problems and findings. *Anthropological Linguistics* 15:406–26.

———. 1975. Mexican Spanish /-s/ in relation to Aztec influence. *SIL* 25:55–61.

———. 1976*a*. Theories of language borrowing tested by American Spanish phonology. *Romance Philology* 30:331–42.

———. 1976*b*. Vowel indistinction and splitting in American Spanish:

Internally derived or externally motivated? *Orbis* 25:280–97.

———. 1977. La influencia maya en la fonología del español de Yucatán. *Anuario de Letras* 15:95–113.

Cavazos Garza, Israel. 1976. El habla del noreste de México: Comentarios. *Universidad de Nuevo León* 1976:419–26.

Cedergren, Henrietta J. 1978. En torno a la variación de la s final de sílaba en Panamá: Análisis cuantitativo. In *Corrientes actuales en la dialectología del Caribe hispánico: Actas de un simposio,* ed. Humberto López Morales, pp. 35–49. Río Piedras: Universidad de Puerto Rico.

Chasca, Edmund de. 1946. The phonology of the speech of the Negroes in early Spanish drama. *Hispanic Review* 14:322–39.

Chavarría-Aguilar, O. L. 1951. The phonemes of Costa Rican Spanish. *Language* 27:248–53.

Clark y Moreno, Joseph A. 1970. A bibliography of bibliographies relating to Mexican-American studies. *El Grito* 3:25–31.

Cock Hincapié, Olga. 1969. *El seseo en el Nuevo Reino de Granada: 1550–1650.* Bogotá: Instituto Caro y Cuervo.

Cohen, Pedro I. 1964. Apuntes sobre la pronunciación del fonema /s/ en Panamá. *Estudios* (Instituto Nacional de Panamá) 2:86–92.

———. 1971. *Estudios de lingüística descriptiva: Temas panameños.* Panama: University of Panama.

Coltharp, Lurline H. 1965. *The tongue of the Tirilones: A linguistic study of a criminal argot.* University: University of Alabama Press.

Cordasco, Francesco; Bucchioni, Eugene; and Castellanos, Diego. 1972. *Puerto Ricans in the United States mainland: A bibliography of reports, texts, critical studies and related materials.* Totowa, N.J.: Rowan and Littlefield.

Corominas, Juan. 1953. Para la fecha del yeísmo y del lleísmo. *NRFH* 7:81–87.

Corrientes actuales en la dialectología del Caribe hispánico: Actas de un simposio. 1978. Ed. Humberto López Morales. Río Piedras: Universidad de Puerto Rico.

Coseriu, Eugenio, ed. 1968. *Current trends in linguistics: Ibero-American and Caribbean linguistics.* The Hague: Mouton.

Costa Sánchez, Manuel. 1977a. Análisis acústico-articulatorio de las cinco vocales del español hablado en Cuba. *Islas* (Universidad Central de Santa Clara) 57:11–127.

———. 1977b. Descripción de particularidades acústico-articulatorias de algunos sonidos consonánticos del español hablado en Cuba. *Islas* (Universidad Central de Santa Clara) 55/56:3–42.

Craddock, Jerry R. 1973. Spanish in North America. *CTL* 10:305–39.

Crews, Cynthia. 1962. Reflections on Judaeo-Spanish by a Spanish Jew. *Vox Romanica* 20:327–34.

Cuervo, Rufino J. 1867–72. *Apuntaciones críticas sobre el lenguaje bogotano.* Bogotá, Colombia.

———. 1901. El castellano en América. *Bulletin Hispanique* 3:35–62.

———. 1944. *Obras inéditas.* Bogotá: Instituto Caro y Cuervo.

Davis, Jack Emory. 1966. The Spanish of Argentina and Uruguay: An annotated bibliography for 1940–1965. *Orbis* 15:160–89, 442–88.

———. 1968. The Spanish of Argentina and Uruguay: An annotated bibliography for 1940–1965, III, III supplement, IV. *Orbis* 17:232–77, 538, 539–73.

———. 1971a. The Spanish of Argentina and Uruguay: An annotated bibliography for 1940–1965. *Orbis* 20:236–69.

———. 1971b. The Spanish of Mexico: An annotated bibliography for 1940–1969. *Hispania* 54:624–56.

Decker, Bob Dan. 1952. Phonology of the Puerto Rican Spanish of Lorain, Ohio: A study in the environmental displacement of a dialect. M.A. thesis, Ohio State University.

Delattre, Pierre; Olsen, C.; and Poenack, E. 1962. A comparative study of declarative intonation in American English and Spanish. *Hispania* 45:233–41.

Del Rosario, Rubén. 1946. La lengua de Puerto Rico. *Asomante* 2:95–103.

———. 1955. *La lengua en Puerto Rico: Ensayos.* New York: Américas.

———. 1958. *Consideraciones sobre la lengua en Puerto Rico.* San Juan.

———. 1970. *El español de América.* Sharon, Conn.: Troutman Press.

———. 1971. La investigación dialectal en Puerto Rico. *Revista de Estudios Hispánicos* 1:9–12.

Doman, Mary G. 1969. "H" aspirada y "f" moderna en el español americano. *Thesaurus* 24:426–58.

Donni de Mirande, Nélida. 1967. Recursos afectivos en el habla de Rosario. *Publicación de la Universidad Nacional del Litoral* 72:247–88.

———. 1968. *El español hablado en Rosario.* Rosario, Argentina: Universidad Nacional del Litoral.

———. 1972. Diferencias internas en el español del sur del litoral argentino. *Revista Española de Lingüística* 2:273–83.

———. 1974. Grupos consonánticos en Rosario. *Thesaurus* 29:526–38.

El español en Puerto Rico: Bibliografía. 1971. *Revista de Estudios Hispánicos* 1:111-24.

Elizaincín, Adolfo. 1976. The emergence of bilingual dialects on the Brazilian-Uruguayan border. *Linguistics* 177:123-34.

Escobar, Alberto. 1976. Bilingualism and dialectology in Peru. *Linguistics* 177:85-96.

———. 1977. ¿Existe el castellano limeño? *Lexis* 1:39-49.

Espinosa, Aurelio M. 1909. Studies in New Mexican Spanish. Part 1. Phonology. *Bulletin of the University of New Mexico* 1:47-162.

———. 1930. *Estudios sobre el español de Nuevo Méjico.* Part 1. *Fonética.* Trans. and rev. by Amado Alonso and Angel Rosenblat. Buenos Aires: Boletín de Dialectología Hispanoamericano. Vol. I: 19-313.

Estrugo, José M. 1958. *Los sefardíes.* Havana.

Estudios sobre el español hablado en las principales ciudades de América. 1977. Ed. Juan Lope Blanch. Mexico: Universidad Nacional Autónoma de México.

Fernández-Shaw, Carlos M. 1972. *Presencia española en los Estados Unidos.* Madrid: Ediciones Cultura Hispánica.

Figueroa Berríos, Edwin. 1971. Habla y folklore en Ponce. *Revista de Estudios Hispánicos* 1:53-74.

Fishman, Joshua A., and Herasimchuk, Eleanor. 1969. The multiple prediction of phonological variables in a bilingual speech community. *American Anthropologist* 71:648-57.

Flórez, Luis. 1950. Del castellano en Colombia: El habla del Chocó. *Boletín del Instituto Caro y Cuervo* 6:110-16.

———. 1951a. El español hablado en Segovia y Remedios. *Boletín del Instituto Caro y Cuervo* 7:18-110.

———. 1951b. *La pronunciación del español en Bogotá.* Bogotá: Instituto Caro y Cuervo.

———. 1957. *Habla y cultura popular en Antioquia.* Bogotá: Instituto Caro y Cuervo.

———. 1960a. El Atlas Lingüístico-Etnográfico de Colombia (ALEC): Nota informativa. Bogotá: Instituto Caro y Cuervo.

———. 1960b. Del habla popular en Santander. *RCF* 2:9-14.

———. 1964. El español hablado en Colombia y su atlas lingüístico. In *Presente y futuro de la lengua española,* 1:5-77. Madrid: OFINES.

———. 1965. *El español hablado en Santander.* Bogotá: Instituto Caro y Cuervo.

———. 1969. *El español hablado en el Departamento del Norte de Santander.* Bogotá: Instituto Caro y Cuervo.

———. 1978. Sobre algunas formas de pronunciar muchos colombianos el español: Datos y problemas. *Thesaurus* 33:197–246.

Fody, Michael, III. 1971. The Spanish of the American Southwest and Louisiana: A bibliographical survey for 1954–1969. *Orbis* 20:529–40.

Fontanella, María B. 1966. Comparación de dos entonaciones regionales argentinas. *Thesaurus* 21:3–15.

———. 1967. La "s" postapical bonaerense. *Thesaurus* 22:394–400.

Fontanella de Weinberg, María B. 1971. La entonación del español de Córdoba, Argentina. *Thesaurus* 25:11–21.

———. 1973. El rehilamiento bonaerense a fines del siglo XVIII. *Thesaurus* 28:338–43.

———. 1974*a*. Aspectos sociolingüísticos del uso de -s en el español bonaerense. *Orbis* 23:85–98.

———. 1974*b*. Comportamiento ante -s de hablantes femeninos y masculinos del español bonaerense. *Romance Philology* 28:50–58.

Gandolfo, Adriana. 1964. Spanish *ll* and *rr* in Buenos Aires and Corrientes. *Proceedings of International Congress of Linguists, Cambridge, Mass., 1962,* pp. 212–16.

Gáspari, Luis de. 1964. Presente y futuro de la lengua española en el Paraguay. In *Presente y futuro de la lengua española,* 1:121–33. Madrid: OFINES.

Gili Gaya, Samuel. 1966. *Nuestra lengua materna.* San Juan: Instituto de Cultura Puertorriqueña.

González, Gustavo. 1969. *The phonology of Corpus Christi Spanish.* Austin: Southwest Educational Development Laboratory.

———. 1973. The analysis of Chicano Spanish and the problem of usage: A critique of "Chicano Spanish dialects and education." *Aztlán* 3:223–31.

Gordon, Alan M. 1979. Notas sobre la fonética del castellano en Bolivia. *Actas, Congreso Internacional de Hispanistas* (Toronto, 1979).

Granda, Germán de. 1966. La velarización de "rr" en el español de Puerto Rico. *RFE* 49:181–227.

———. 1968. *Transculturación e interferencia lingüística en el Puerto Rico contemporáneo: 1898–1968.* Bogotá: Instituto Caro y Cuervo.

———. 1969. La desfonologización de /R/ - /R̄/ en el dominio lingüístico hispano. *Boletín del Instituto Caro y Cuervo* 24:1–11.

———. 1973. Dialectología, historia social y sociología lingüística en Iscuande, Depto. de Nariño, Colombia. *Thesaurus* 28:445–70.

———. 1977. *Estudios sobre un área dialectal hispanoamericana de población negra: Las tierras bajas occidentales de Colombia.* Bogotá: Instituto Caro y Cuervo.

Guitart, Jorge Miguel. 1976. *Markedness and a Cuban dialect of Spanish.* Washington, D.C.: Georgetown University Press.

——. 1978. A propósito del español de Cuba y Puerto Rico: Hacia un modelo sociolingüístico de lo sociodialectal. In *Corrientes actuales en la dialectología del Caribe hispánico: Actas de un simposio,* ed. Humberto López Morales, pp. 77–92. Río Piedras: Universidad de Puerto Rico.

Guitarte, Guillermo. 1955. El ensordecimiento del žeísmo porteño. *RFE* 39:261–83.

——. 1958. Cuervo, Henríquez Ureña y la polémica sobre el andalucismo de América. *Vox Románica* 17:363–416. Reprinted in *Boletín del Instituto Caro y Cuervo* 14 (1959):20–81.

——. 1969. Para una historia del español en América basada en documentos: El seseo en el Nuevo Reino de Granada, 1550–1650. In *Programa Interamericano de Lingüística y Ensañanza de Idiomas: Simposio de México,* pp. 191–99. Mexico: Universidad Nacional Autónoma de México.

——. 1971. Notas para la historia del yeísmo. In *Sprache und Geschichte: Festschrift für Harri Meier zum 65 Geburtstag,* pp. 179–98. Munich.

——. 1974. Proyecto de estudio histórico del español americano. *El Simposio de San Juan, P.R., junio de 1971* (San Juan: Depto. de Instrucción Pública), pp. 169–72.

Gutiérrez Eskildsen, Rosario M. 1933–34. Cómo hablamos en Tabasco. *Investigaciones lingüísticas* (Mexico: Instituto Mexicano de Investigaciones Lingüísticas) 1:265–312.

——. 1936–37. El lenguaje popular en Jalisco. *Investigaciones Lingüísticas* (Mexico: Instituto Mexicano de Investigaciones Lingüísticas) 4:191–211.

Haden, Ernest F., and Matluck, Joseph. 1973. El habla culta de la Habana: Análisis fonológico preliminar. *Anuario de Letras* 2:5–33.

Hammond, Robert M. 1978. An experimental verification of the phonemic status of open and closed vowels in Caribbean Spanish. In *Corrientes actuales en la dialectología del Caribe hispánico: Actas de un simposio,* ed. Humberto López Morales, pp. 93–143. Río Piedras: Universidad de Puerto Rico.

Hannum, Thomasina. 1978. Attitudes of bilingual students toward Spanish. *Hispania* 61:90–94.

Harris, James W. 1969. *Spanish phonology.* Cambridge: MIT Press.

——. 1974. Morphologization of phonological rules: An example from Chicano Spanish. In *Linguistic studies in Romance languages,* pp. 8–27. Washington: Georgetown University Press.

———. 1979. Voiced versus plus voice in Spanish obstruents. *Hispania* 62:342–44.

Hauser, Guido. 1947. La pronunciación del castellano en Venezuela: Un reflejo de la continuidad romance. *Revista de Educación y Magisterio* (Caracas), 8–9:50–52, 95–104.

Henríquez Ureña, Pedro. 1921. Comienzos del español en América. *RFE* 8:357–90; 17 (1930): 227–84; 18 (1931): 120–48.

———. 1925. El supuesto andalucismo de América. *Boletín* (Buenos Aires: *Cuadernos del Instituto de Filología*) 2:117–22.

———. 1940. *El español en Santo Domingo.* Buenos Aires: Casa Editora Coni.

Herrero Fuentes, Ignacio. 1944. El castellano en Panamá. *Universidad* (Revista de la Universidad Interamericana, Panamá) 22:81–101.

Hills, Elijah Clarence. 1906. New Mexican Spanish. *PMLA* 21:706–53.

Hirsch, Ruth. 1951. A study of some aspects of a Judeo-Spanish dialect as spoken by a New York Sephardic family. Ph.D. diss., University of Michigan.

Honsa, Vladimir. 1965. The phonemic system of Argentinian Spanish. *Hispania* 48:275–83.

———. 1975. Clasificación de los dialectos españoles de América y la estructura de los dialectos de Colombia. In *Actas del Simposio de Montevideo,* pp. 196–209. Mexico: Editorial Galache.

Hyman, Ruth. 1956. ŋ as an allophone denoting open juncture in several Spanish American dialects. *Hispania* 39:293–99.

Ibaseşcu, Cristina. 1965. Peculiaridades fonéticas del español de Cuba. *Revue Roumaine de Linguistique* 10:571–94.

———. 1968a. *El español en Cuba: Observaciones fonéticas y fonológicas.* Bucharest: Sociedad Rumana de Lingüística Románica.

———. 1968b. Sobre la existencia de una fricativa labiodental sonora en el español cubano. *Actas* (Mexico: Congreso Internacional de Hispanistas) 3:473–78.

Jiménez Sabater, Maximiliano A. 1975. *Más datos sobre el español de República Dominicana.* Santo Domingo: Instituto Tecnológico de Santo Domingo.

———. 1977. Estructuras morfosintácticas en el español dominicano: Algunas implicaciones sociolingüísticas. *Ciencia y sociedad* 2:5–19. Reprinted in *Corrientes actuales en la dialectología del Caribe hispánico: Actas de un simposio,* ed. Humberto López Morales, pp. 165–80. Río Piedras: Universidad de Puerto Rico, 1978.

Jorge Morel, Elercia. 1974. *Estudio lingüístico de Santo Domingo: Aportación a la geografía lingüística del Caribe e Hispano América.* Santo Domingo: Editora Taller.

King, Harold V. 1952. Outline of Mexican Spanish phonology. *Studies in Linguistics* (Arlington, Va.) 10:51–62.

———. 1953. Sketch of Guayaquil Spanish phonology. *Studia Linguistica* 61:26–30.

Kvavik, Karen. 1976. Research and pedagogical materials on Spanish intonation: A re-examination. *Hispania* 59:406–17.

———. 1978. Directions in recent Spanish intonation analysis. In *Corrientes actuales en la dialectología del Caribe hispánico: Actas de un simposio,* ed. Humberto López Morales, pp. 181–97. Río Piedras: Universidad de Puerto Rico.

Kvavik, Karen H., and Olson, C. L. 1974. Theories and methods in Spanish intonational studies: Survey. *Phonetica* 30:65–100.

Lacayo, Heberto. 1954. Apuntes sobre la pronunciación del español en Nicaragua. *Hispania* 37:267–68.

———. 1962. *Cómo pronuncian el español en Nicaragua.* Mexico: Universidad Iberoamericana.

Lagmanovich, David. 1957. Sobre el español de Santiago del Estero. *Revista de la Facultad de Filosofía y Letras* 3:55–70.

———. 1976. La pronunciación del español en Tucumán, Argentina, a través de algunos textos dialectales. *Orbis* 25:298–315.

Lamb, Anthony J. 1968. A phonological study of the Spanish of Havana, Cuba. Ph.D. diss., University of Kansas.

Lapesa, Rafael. 1956. Sobre el ceceo y el seseo en Hispanoamérica. *Revista Iberoamericana* 21:409–16.

———. 1964. El andaluz y el español de América. In *Presente y futuro de la lengua española,* 1:173–82. Madrid: OFINES.

———. 1980. *Historia de la lengua española.* 8th edition. Madrid: Gredos.

Lihani, John. 1968. Observations on the Spanish of South America. *Kentucky Romance Quarterly* 15:95–117.

Lope Blanch, Juan M. 1966. En torno a las vocales caedizas del español mexicano. *NRFH* 17:1–19.

———. 1966–67. Sobre el rehilamiento de ll/y en México. *Anuario de Letras* 6:43–60.

———. 1967. La -r final del español mexicano y el sustrato nahua. *Thesaurus* 22:1–20.

———. 1968. Hispanic dialectology: Spanish-American studies. In *Current trends in linguistics,* pp. 106–57. The Hague: Mouton.

———. 1969. Para la delimitación de las zonas dialectales de México. In *El simposio de México: Actas, informes y comunicaciones,* pp. 255–64. Mexico: Universidad Nacional Autónoma de México.

———. 1972. *Estudios sobre el español de México.* Mexico: Universidad Nacional Autónoma de México.

———. 1974. Dialectología mexicana y sociolingüística. *NRFH* 23:1–34.

———. 1975. Un caso de posible influencia maya en el español mexicano. *NRFH* 24:89–100.

López Morales, Humberto. 1968. El español de Cuba: Situación bibliográfica. *RFE* 51:111–37.

Luria, Max A. 1930. Judeo-Spanish dialects in New York City. In *Todd Memorial Volumes,* 2:7–16. New York: Columbia University Press.

MacCurdy, Raymond R. 1950. *The Spanish dialect of St. Bernard Parish, Louisiana.* Albuquerque: University of New Mexico Press.

MacPherson, Ian Richard. 1975. *Spanish phonology: Descriptive and historical.* Manchester, England: Manchester University Press; New York: Barnes and Noble.

Malmberg, Bertil. 1947. *Notas sobre la fonética del español en el Paraguay.* Lund: Yearbook of the New Society of Letters.

———. 1947. L'espagnol dans le Nouveau Monde: Problème de linguistique générale. *Studia Linguistica* 1:79–116; 2 (1948):1–36.

———. 1950. *Etudes sur la phonétique de l'espagnol parlé en Argentine.* Etudes Romanes de Lund publiées par Alf Lombard, 10. Lund: Alf Lombard.

———. 1952. Le "r" final en espagnol mexicain. *Estudios Dedicados a Menéndez Pidal* 3:131–34.

———. 1964a. Tradición hispánica e influencia indígena en la fonética hispanoamericana. In *Presente y futuro de la lengua española,* 2:227–45. Madrid: OFINES.

———. 1964b. Notes sur la structure syllabique de l'espagnol mexicain. *Zeitschrift für Phonetik Sprachwissenschaft und Kommunikationsforschung* 17:251–55.

———. 1972. Descripción y clasificación: A propósito de las semivocales castellanas. In *Studia hispanica in honorem R. Lapesa,* 1:413–15. Madrid: Gredos.

Marden, Charles. 1896. *The phonology of the Spanish dialect of Mexico City.* Baltimore: Johns Hopkins University Press.

Marrocco, Mary Ann Wilkinson. 1972. The Spanish of Corpus Christi. Ph.D. diss., University of Illinois.

Matluck, Joseph. 1951. *La pronunciación en el español del Valle de México.* Mexico: Universidad Nacional Autónoma de México.

———. 1952. La pronunciación del español en el Valle de México. *NRFH* 6:109–20.

——. 1961. Fonemas finales en el consonantismo puertorriqueño. *NRFH* 15:332–42.

——. 1963. La *é* trabada en la ciudad de México. *Anuario de Letras* 3:5–34.

——. 1965. Entonación hispánica. *Anuario de Letras* 5:5–32.

Matluck, Joseph, and Mace, Betty J. 1973. Language characteristics of Mexican-American children: Implications for assessment, *Journal of Speech Psychology* 11:365–86.

Megenney, William W. 1978. El problema de "R" velar en Puerto Rico. *Thesaurus* 33:72–86.

Mel'cuk, I. A. 1973. On the phonemic status of semivowels in Spanish. *Linguistics* 109:35–60.

Menéndez Pidal, Ramón. 1957–58. Sevilla frente a Madrid. In *A André Martinet: Estructuralismo e historia,* 3:99–165. La Laguna: Universidad de la Laguna.

México. Universidad Nacional. Centro de Lingüística. 1976. *El habla popular de la Ciudad de México.* Mexico: Universidad Nacional Autónoma de México.

Montes Giraldo, José J. 1959. Del español hablado en Bolívar, Colombia. *Boletín del Instituto Caro y Cuervo* 14:82–110.

——. 1962. Sobre el habla de San Basilio de Palenque. *Boletín del Instituto Caro y Cuervo* 17:446–50.

——. 1966. Observaciones sobre el español en Montevideo. *Noticias Culturales* (Bogotá: Instituto Caro y Cuervo) 65:1–4.

——. 1967. El atlas lingüístico etnográfico de Colombia (ALEC): Encuestas, exploradores, publicaciones, 1956–1966. *Thesaurus* 22: 94–100.

——. 1969. ¿Desaparece la "ll" de la pronunciación bogotana? *Thesaurus* 24:102–4.

——. 1970. *Dialectología y geografía lingüística: Notas de orientación.* Bogotá: Instituto Caro y Cuervo.

——. 1971. Acerca de la apropiación por el niño del sistema fonológico español. *Thesaurus* 26:323–46.

——. 1974. El habla del Chocó. *Thesaurus* 29:409–28.

——. 1975*a.* Breves notas de fonética actual del español. *Thesaurus* 30:338–39.

——. 1975*b.* La neutralización del consonantismo implosivo en un habla colombiana—Mechengue, Cauca. *Thesaurus* 30:561–85.

Navarro Maraví, Aurelio R. 1964. La pronunciación en los pueblos del centro del Perú. *Revista de Educación* (Huancayo: Universidad Nacional del Centro) 1:145–47.

Navarro Tomás, Tomás. 1933. La frontera del andaluz. *Revista de Fi-lología española* 20:225-77.

———. 1943. *Cuestionario lingüístico hispanoamericano.* Buenos Aires: Instituto de Filología. 2d ed., 1945.

———. 1944. *Manual de entonación española.* New York: Hispanic Institute in the United States.

———. 1948. *El español en Puerto Rico.* Río Piedras: Universidad de Puerto Rico.

———. 1949. The old aspirated "h" in Spain and in the Spanish of America. *Word* 5:166-69.

———. 1956. Apuntes sobre el español dominicano. *Revista Ibero-americana* 21:417-28.

———. 1957. *Manual de pronunciación española.* 5th ed. New York: Hafner.

———. 1962. Muestra del ALPI. *NRFH* 16:1-15.

———. 1974. Transcripción estrecha. *Anglia* (Mexico: Universidad Nacional Autónoma de México) 12:181-87.

Nebrija, Antonio de. 1977. *Reglas de orthographia en la lengua castellana: Estudio y edición de Antonio Quilis.* Bogotá: Instituto Caro y Cuervo.

Nichols, Madaline. 1941. *A bibliographical guide to materials on American Spanish.* Cambridge: Harvard University Press.

Nykl, Aloys. 1930. Notes on the Spanish of Yucatán, Veracruz and Tlaxcala. *Modern Philology* 27:451-60.

Obaid, Antonio H. 1973. The vagaries of Spanish "S." *Hispania* 56: 60-67.

Ocampo Marín, Jaime. 1968. *Notas sobre el español hablado en Mérida.* Merida, Venezuela: Universidad de los Andes, Facultad de Humanidades y Educación.

Olsted, David. 1954. A note on the dialect of Regla, Cuba. *Hispania* 37:293-94.

Ornstein, Jacob. 1971. Language varieties along the United States-Mexican border. In *Application of linguistics: Selected papers of the Second International Congress of Applied Linguistics,* ed. Perren and Trim, pp. 349-62. Cambridge: Cambridge University Press.

———. 1972. Toward a classification of southwest Spanish nonstandard variants. *Linguistics* 93:70-87.

Oroz, Rodolfo. 1964. El español de Chile. In *Presente y futuro de la lengua española,* 1:93-109. Madrid: OFINES.

———. 1966. *La lengua castellana en Chile.* Santiago: Universidad de Chile.

Perissinotto, Giorgio Sabino Antonio. 1975. *Fonología del español ha-*

blado en la Ciudad de México: Ensayo de un método sociolingüístico. Mexico: Colegio de México.

Phillips, Robert N., Jr. 1967. Los Angeles Spanish: A descriptive analysis. Ph.D. diss., University of Wisconsin.

———. 1972. The influence of English on the /v/ in Los Angeles Spanish. In *Studies in language and linguistics,* 1972–73, ed. Ralph W. Ewton and Jacob Ornstein, pp. 201–12. El Paso: Texas Western Press.

———. 1975. Southwestern Spanish: A descriptive analysis. In *Hispanic influence in the United States,* pp. 5–13. New York: Spanish Institute.

Post, Anita C. 1934. Southern Arizona Spanish phonology. *University of Arizona Humanities Bulletin,* no. 5.

Poulter, Virgil L. 1973. A phonological study of the Spanish speech of Mexican-American college students native to Ft. Worth–Dallas. Ph.D. diss., Lousiana State University.

Predmore, Richard L. 1945. La pronunciación de varias consonantes en el español de Guatemala. *Revista de Filología Hispánica* 7:277–80.

Quilis, Antonio. 1963. *Fonética y fonología del español.* Madrid: Gredos.

———. 1964. La juntura en español: Un problema de fonología. In *Presente y futuro de la lengua española,* 2:163–71. Madrid: OFINES.

Rabanales, Ambrosio. 1960. Hiato y antihiato en el español vulgar de Chile. *Boletín de Filología de la Universidad de Chile* 12:197–223.

———. 1964. Pasado y presente de la investigación lingüística y filológica en Chile. *Boletín de Filología* (Santiago: Universidad de Chile) 16:121–43.

Rael, Juan B. 1937. A study of the phonology and morphology of New Mexican Spanish based on a collection of 410 folk-tales. Ph.D. diss., Stanford University.

Reinecke, John E.; Tsuzaki, Stanley M.; Decamp, David; Hancock, Ian; and Wood, Richard E. 1975. *A bibliography of pidgin and Creole languages.* Honolulu: University of Hawaii.

Resnick, Melvyn C. 1975. *Phonological variants and dialect identification in Latin American Spanish.* The Hague: Mouton.

———. 1976. Algunos aspectos histórico-geográficos de la dialectología hispanoamericana. *Orbis* 25:264–76.

Revilla, Angel. 1976. Los panameñismos: ¿Una nueva lengua en formación? *LA* 5:121–30.

Ricci, Julio. 1967. The influence of locally spoken Italian dialects on

River Plate Spanish. *Forum Italicum* (Tallahassee, Fla.: South Atlantic AATI) 1:48–59.

Robe, Stanley. 1948. "l" and "r" implosivas en el español de Panamá. *NRFH* 2:272–75.

———. 1960. *The Spanish of rural Panama: Major dialectal features.* Berkeley: University of California Press.

Rodríguez del Pino, Salvador. 1973. El idioma de Aztlán: Una lengua que surge. *Universidad de México* 27:16–19.

Rona, José Pedro. 1963. La frontera lingüística entre el portugués y el español en el norte del Uruguay. *Veritas* (Porto Alegre, Brazil: Revista Pontífica Universidad Católica) 8:201–19.

———. 1964. El problema de la división del español americano en zonas dialectales. In *Presente y futuro de la lengua española,* 1:215–26. Madrid: OFINES.

Rosenblat, Angel. 1964. Base del español de América: Nivel social y cultural de los conquistadores y pobladores. *Boletín de Filología* (Santiago: Universidad de Chile) 16:171–230.

———. 1977. *Los conquistadores y su lengua.* Caracas: Universidad Central.

Rosell, A. 1978. Sobre dialectología uruguaya. *Revista de la Biblioteca Nacional* 18:263–95.

Rubin, Joan. 1968*a.* Bilingual usage in Paraguay. In *Readings in the sociology of language,* ed. Joshua A. Fishman, pp. 513–30. The Hague: Mouton.

———. 1968*b. National bilingualism in Paraguay.* The Hague: Mouton.

———. 1968*c.* Language and education in Paraguay. In *Language problems of the developing nations,* ed. Charles A. Ferguson and Jyotirinda Das Gupta. New York: John Wiley.

Sala, Marius. 1972. Los fonemas /š/, /ž/ en el judeoespañol. In *Studia hispanica in honorem R. Lapesa,* 1:521–24. Madrid: Gredos.

Sanabria Fernández, Hernando. 1965. El habla popular de la provincia de Valle Grande (Departamento de Santa Cruz), Bolivia. *Revista de la Universidad Autónoma "Gabriel René Moreno"* (Santa Cruz, Bolivia), separata of nos. 16–22.

Saporta, Sol. 1956. A note on Spanish semivowels. *Language* 32:287–90.

Serís, Homero. 1964. *Bibliografía de la lingüística española.* Bogotá: Instituto Caro y Cuervo.

Solé, Carlos A. 1970. *Bibliografía sobre el español en América: 1920–1967.* Washington, D.C.: Georgetown University Press.

———. 1972. Bibliografía sobre el español en América: 1920–1967. *Anuario de Letras* 10:253–88.

———. 1975. El español en los Estados Unidos: Perspectiva sociolingüística. *Thesaurus* 20:318–37.

Spaulding, Robert, and Patt, Beatrice. 1948. Data for the chronology of "theta" and "jota." *Hispanic Review* 16:50–60.

Spyropoulos, Esperanza M. 1969. The phonology of the word in a Spanish dialect [Ballez, Chihuahua, Mexico]. *Language and Linguistics* (Washington, D.C.: Georgetown University) 4:24–41.

Stockwell, Robert P.; Bowen, J. Donald; and Silva-Fuenzalida, I. 1956. Spanish juncture and intonation. *Language* 32:641–65.

Suárez, Víctor M. 1945. *El español que se habla en Yucatán: Apuntamientos filológicos.* Mérida, Yucatán: Diaz Massa.

Terrell, Tracy D. 1975*a*. Functional constraints on deletion of word final /s/ in Cuban Spanish. *Berkeley Linguistics Society* 1:431–37.

———. 1975*b*. La nasal implosiva y final en el español de Cuba. *Anuario de Letras* 13:257–71.

———. 1977*a*. La aspiración y elisión en el español cubano. In *Estudios sobre el español hablado en las principales ciudades de América,* ed. Juan Lope Branch. Mexico: Universidad Nacional Autónoma de México.

———. 1977*b*. Aspiration and deletion of word final /s/ in the Spanish of Caracas, Venezuela. Paper, Hispanic Colloquium, University of Hawaii, July 1977.

———. 1978*a*. Aportación de los estudios dialectales antillanas a la teoría fonológica. In *Corrientes actuales en la dialectología del Caribe hispánico: Actas de un simposio,* ed. Humberto López Morales, pp. 217–37. Río Piedras: Universidad de Puerto Rico.

———. 1978*b*. Sobre la aspiración y elisión de /S/ implosiva y final en el español de Puerto Rico. *Nueva Revista de filología hispánica* 37:24–38.

Teschner, Richard V.; Bills, Garland D.; and Craddock, Jerry R. 1975. *Spanish and English of the United States Hispanos: A critical, annotated, linguistic bibliography.* Arlington, Va.: Center for Applied Linguistics.

Toscano Mateus, Humberto. 1953. El español en el Ecuador. *Revista de Filología Española,* suppl. 65 (Madrid).

———. 1964. El español hablado en el Ecuador. In *Presente y futuro de la lengua española,* 1:111–25. Madrid: OFINES.

Tsuzaki, Stanley M. 1963. English influence in the phonology and morphology of the Spanish spoken in the Mexican colony in Detroit. Ph.D. diss., University of Michigan.

Umphrey, C. W., and Adatto, Emma. 1936. Linguistic archaism of the Seattle Sephardim. *Hispania* 19:255–64.

Valdés Fallis, Guadalupe. 1978. A comprehensive approach to the teaching of Spanish to bilingual Spanish-speaking students. *Modern Language Journal* 62:102–10.

Vallejo-Claros, Bernardo. 1970. La distribución y estratificación de /r/ /r̄/ /s/ en el español cubano. Ph.D. diss., University of Texas, Austin.

Van Wijk, H. L. 1961. Los bolivianismos fonéticos en la obra costumbrista de Alfredo Guillén Pinto. *Boletín de Filología* (Santiago: Universidad de Chile) 13:49–73.

Vaquero de Ramírez, María T. 1971. Estudio lingüístico de Barranquitas. *Revista de Estudios Hispánicos* 1:23–38.

————. 1978. Hacia una espectrografía dialectal: El fonema /č/ en Puerto Rico. In *Corrientes actuales en la dialectología del Caribe hispánico: Actas de un simposio,* ed. Humberto López Morales, pp. 239–47. Río Piedras: Universidad de Puerto Rico.

Varas Reyes, Víctor. 1960. *El castellano popular en Tarija.* La Paz: Talleres Gráficos.

Vásquez, Washington. 1953. El fonema /s/ en el español del Uruguay. *Revista de la Facultad de Humanidades y Ciencias* (Montevideo: Universidad del Uruguay) 10:87–94.

Vidal de Battini, Berta E. 1949. *El habla rural de San Luis. 1. Fonética, morfología, sintaxis.* Buenos Aires: Instituto de Filología.

————. 1964a. *El español de la Argentina.* Buenos Aires: Consejo Nacional de Educación.

————. 1964b. El español de la Argentina. In *Presente y futuro de la lengua española,* 1:183–92. Madrid: OFINES.

Wagner, Max L. 1920. Amerikanisch-Spanisch und Vulgärlatein. *ZRPh* 40:286–312, 385–404.

————. 1927. El supuesto andalucismo de América y la teoría climatológica. *RFE* 14:20–32.

Willey, Norman. 1926. "c" and "z" in American Spanish. *Philological Quarterly* 5:306–24.

Wilson, Jack Leroy. 1971. A generative phonological study of Costa Rica Spanish. Ph.D. diss., University of Michigan.

Wolf, C., and Jiménez, E. 1977. El yeísmo porteño. In *Estudios sobre el español hablado en las principales ciudades de América,* ed. Juan Lope Branch. Mexico: Universidad Nacional Autónoma de México.

Woodbridge, Hensley C. 1977. Fourteen Chicano bibliographies, 1971–1975. *Modern Language Journal* 61:20–25.

Wright, Leavit O., and Robe, Stanley. 1939. Final consonant plus "n"-glide in Jalisco, Mexico. *Modern Language Notes* 54:439–42; also in *PMLA* 52 (1955):561

Young, Ronald. 1972. El habla de Alto Lucero Pacheco, Veracruz. Ph.D. diss., University of Illinois.

———. 1977. Rehilamiento of /y/ in Spanish. *Hispania* 60:327–30.

Zapata Arellano, Rodrigo. 1975. Nota sobre la articulación del fonema /f/ en el español de Chile. *Signos* 8:131–33.

Zlotchew, Clark M. 1971. Recurrent phonetic developments in the Spanish consonant. *Orbis* 20:436–46.

———. 1974. The transformation of the multiple vibrant to the fricative velar in the Spanish of Puerto Rico. *Orbis* 23:81–84.

Index

Accessibility, as factor in language development, 2
Acento de intensidad, 18
Acento melódico, 18
-ado, treatment of, 36, 51, 67, 73
Agüero, Arturo, 39
Albor, Hugo, 6, 19, 34, 36, 38
ALEC (Atlas lingüístico etnográfico de Colombia), 20, 37
Antiplano (Bolivia), 28
Alvar, Manuel, viii, 62
Alvarado de Ricord, Elsie, viii, 67
Andalusian Castilian, as factor in American Spanish, 2, 5, 6, 9, 20, 76, 80, 84
Antioquia (Colombia), 4, 36
Arizona, 81
Aspiration. *See* /s/
Assibilation. *See* /ř/
Atlantic coast (Colombia), 37
Attitudinal phenomena, vii, 24, 48, 65, 67
Azuay (Ecuador), 48

/b, d, g/, occlusive after another consonant or semivowel, 3, 5, 6, 11, 34, 52, 65, 73, 78
Bariloche (Argentina), 24
Beardsley, Theodore S., 81
Bolinger, Dwight L., 18
Border Spanish (U.S.–Mexico), 80, 81
Boyd-Bowman, Peter, 2, 19, 60, 62

c (i, e), z. See /s/
/č/, variations and distribution, 12

/č/ as [š], viii, 42, 67, 78
/č/ as [tj], 37, 78
/č/ as [tś], 31
Cali, 37
California, 81
Cañar (Ecuador), 48
Canary Islands, 84
Canellada de Zamora, María J., 19
Canfield, D. Lincoln, ix, 3, 4, 5, 34, 81
Carchi (Ecuador), 48
Cárdenas, Daniel, 60
Cassano, Paul, 70
Castilian continuum, vii, 1, 3
Ceceo, 4
Chaco (Argentina), 24
Chicago, 84
Cock Hincapié, Olga, 4
Colegio de México, 60
Combinaciones cultas, 54, 65
Córdoba, Fray Juan de, 4
Córdoba (Argentina), 24
Corrientes (Argentina), 88
Costeño, mode of articulation, 31, 34, 48, 51, 52
Cundinamarca (Colombia), 34
Cuyanos (Argentina), 23

/d/, occlusive after consonant. *See* /b, d, g/
/d/, variations and distribution, 11
-/d/- as [r], 37
-/d/- as [t], 67
Davis, Jack, ix
Delattre, Pierre, 19
Donni de Mirande, Nélida, vii, 23, 24
Dzhudezmo, 84

115